mended 8/24/06 A.P.

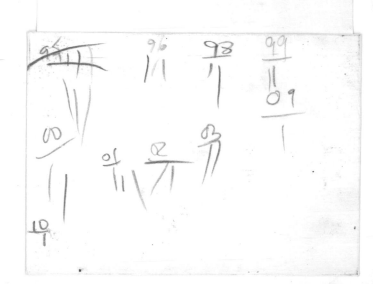

1/95

The MEXICAN REVOLUTION 1910-1920

. . . . .

R. Conrad Stein

New Discovery Books
New York

Maxwell Macmillan Canada
Toronto

Maxwell Macmillan International
New York Oxford Singapore Sydney

Design: Deborah Fillion
Photo research: Robert C. Somerlott

New Discovery Books
Macmillan Publishing Company
866 Third Avenue
New York, NY 10022

Maxwell Macmillan Canada, Inc.
1200 Eglinton Avenue East
Suite 200
Don Mills, Ontario M3C 3N1

Macmillan Publishing Company is part of the Maxwell
Communication Group of Companies.

First edition

Printed in the United States of America

10 9 8 7 6 5 4 3 2 1

Library of Congress Cataloging-in-Publication Data
Stein, R. Conrad
    The Mexican Revolution, 1910–1920 / R. Conrad Stein. 1st ed.
      p. cm.
    "A Timestop book."
    Includes bibliographical references.
    Summary: Presents a history of the struggle for political control in
Mexico during the years 1910 to 1920, including biographical
sketches of key personalities.
    ISBN 0-02-786950-4
    1. Mexico—History—Revolution, 1910–1920—Juvenile
literature. 2. Mexico—History—Revolution, 1910–1920—
Biography—Juvenile literature. 3. Mexico—Biography—Juvenile
literature. [1. Mexico—History—Revolution, 1910–1920.
2. Mexico—Biography.]
    I. Title.
F1234.S84 1994
972.08'16—dc20   93-17259

CONTENTS

5   Introductory Note

7   Introduction: Messages from the Gods

11   Chapter 1: The Díaz Years

25   Chapter 2: The Gathering Storm

41   Chapter 3: Madero

55   Chapter 4: The Ten Tragic Days

67   Chapter 5: Huerta

79   Chapter 6: War Consumes Mexico

93   Chapter 7: General versus General

111 Chapter 8: The Twilight of the Generals

121 Chapter 9: A New Society

135 Chapter 10: In the Wake of War

145 *Chronology of the Mexican Revolution*

151 *Biographical Sketches of the Mexican Revolution*

156 *For Further Information*

158 *Index*

Death rides over the Mexican landscape in this engraving depicting the tragedy of the Mexican Revolution.

Introductory Note

War is cruel and there is no way to refine it.

*—American general William
Tecumseh Sherman*

ertainly a cruel war was the Mexican Revolution, fought from 1910 to 1920. It was a civil
war that pitted rich against poor and white
against nonwhite. During the decade-long conflict, hatred fed upon hatred and the land became a
slaughterhouse. As many as two million people died in
the fighting and from the diseases and famine brought
about by warfare.

But the brutality unleashed by the war in no way
reflects the temperament of the Mexican people. Anyone
who has lived in the country knows their warmth and
gentleness. Rather, the Revolution was an uncharacteris-

tic period of naked violence. The explosion of violence came about after decades of simmering frustrations finally boiled over like a stew left too long on the fire. The Mexican philosopher Octavio Paz described the Revolution as "an excess and a squandering, an explosion of joy and of hopelessness…of suicide and life, all of them mixed together."

INTRODUCTION:
MESSAGES FROM
THE GODS

Every moon, every year, every day,
Every wind comes and goes
And all blood reaches its final
Resting place.

—A poem written in ancient Mexico

ong before Europeans came to the New World, the Aztec nation ruled central Mexico. Mystery and magic dominated Aztec thinking. The Aztecs believed that unexplainable events foretold doom for their society. Starting in the early 1500s, the people witnessed a frightening chain of dramatic and mysterious signs. A three-headed comet that baffled Aztec astronomers hung over central Mexico for many nights. An Aztec general claimed he was driven out of a northern province by stones that rained down from the sky. A tem-

A mural by Diego Rivera shows the class division of Mexican society, rooted in the Spanish conquest of the native Indian civilization.

ple that stood on top of the largest pyramid in the Aztec capital (present-day Mexico City) caught fire and burned to ashes despite the frantic efforts of workers to put out the blaze.

Then, in 1519 (the year One Reed on the Aztec calendar), an army of 650 Spaniards landed on Mexico's eastern shores. Commanded by Hernán Cortés, the Spaniards marched inland and captured the Aztec capital. The mighty Aztec nation, whose territories once spread from ocean to ocean and whose armies seemed invincible, never rose again.

For the next 300 years, the flag of Spain waved above Mexico. A new race—the *mestizos*—was born out of intermarriage between white Spaniards and the Aztecs and other Indian peoples. Under Spain, Mexico divided into three classes: the whites of Spanish heritage, who owned most of the land and commanded the wealth; the mestizos, who were given meager privileges by the white ruling class; and the Indians, who were treated as a defeated race and lived in wretched poverty. A War of Independence fought between 1810 and 1820 liberated Mexico from Spanish rule. But the class system, based largely on race, remained in place.

In 1910 Mexicans prepared to celebrate the 100th anniversary of their War of Independence. However, from the planning stage the celebration was marred by troubling events. In Tampico a spectacular pillar of fire shot out of the ground and burned so brilliantly it could be seen for miles. American oil engineers claimed it was simply an out-of-control gusher. Over central Mexico a fiery comet lit up the night sky, frightening cows so badly they refused to give milk. Educated Mexicans knew it was Halley's comet making its regular 76-year visit to earth. But the Indians had their own explanations for the unusual occurrences. They believed, as their ancestors believed 400 years earlier, that these were messages from heaven and they foretold pestilence, famine, war, and death.

In many ways, they would soon turn out to be right.

Chapter 1

The
DIAZ
YEARS

. . . . .

In the year 1910 there was a strongman of the Americas advertised in all the world, and his name was Porfirio Díaz of Mexico.

—Anita Brenner, from her book
The Wind that Swept Mexico

A spiritual bond connects the Mexican soul to the land. The earth is the wellspring of corn, which is in turn made into tortillas, the common bread of Mexico. During the Mexican Revolution that started in 1910, *tierra* (land) was the prize that drove men and women to charge into blazing machine guns. But though land and all the passion it aroused fueled the fighting, the Revolution began when well-meaning men worked to topple a president who had risen amid political chaos and ruled for more than 30 years.

After achieving independence in 1820, Mexico entered a long period of political confusion. Presidents came and went, not by free elections but through military mutinies. During those chaotic years, the gloomy general Antonio Santa Anna was president of Mexico 11 different times over a span of 30 years. Partly because of disorders in the capital, Mexico lost half its territory through a disastrous war with the United States. The nation also endured a four-year occupation by the French. The remarkable president Benito Juárez tried to bring democracy to Mexico, but he was unable to stop the civil wars. Juárez died in office in 1872, and after five years of military manipulating, his onetime trusted lieutenant, Porfirio Díaz, was inaugurated president.

Porfirio Díaz grew up in the southern state of Oaxaca. He was a mestizo of mostly Mixtec Indian blood. His family ran a tiny hotel. As a boy the future president admired the army officers who paraded through his town ramrod straight, riding the finest horses he had ever seen. Early in life Díaz decided to make the army his career. While serving as a junior officer, he proved fearless under fire. Díaz was captured in the war against the French, but he made a daring escape and returned to lead his unit.

Upon becoming president in 1877, Díaz took command of one of the most backward lands on earth. While Europe and the United States had developed extensive factory systems, Mexico lacked even a modern railroad. Latin nations such as Brazil, Argentina, Chile, and Cuba were worlds ahead of Mexico in industrial progress. Nearly six decades of political warfare had cost Mexico its place among the industrial nations. Now Díaz intended to keep the peace in order to forge an industrial future in the country.

To end the savage military mutinies that triggered internal wars, Díaz offered his rivals the choice of *pan o palo* (bread or the club). In effect, he told ambitious politicians and generals: Work with me and you will be rewarded; fight me and you will be beaten down. Ruthlessly and without hesitation he killed military men intent on taking his place as president. When a group of army officers attempted to overthrow him in the 1880s, he grabbed a pad of paper, scratched out a single command, and handed it to his chief of staff. The message read, "Catch in the act; kill on the spot." Still, for the most part, political executions were rare in the Díaz years. Through a program of fear and rewards, he kept rivals far from his throne.

Díaz's political strength grew to envelop the entire nation. Soon all 27 of Mexico's state governors were Díaz's hand-chosen men. Elections were held, but the president's small army of *jefe políticos* (political bosses) stuffed ballot boxes and rigged results. In one state, prisoners in the penitentiary were put to work marking ballots assembly-line fashion and sending them to vote counters. Díaz also exercised absolute control over the Congress in Mexico City. Once he gratefully presented a seat in the House of Representatives to a dentist who had cured his aching tooth.

Democracy, Díaz believed, was an empty dream in a country where only 15 percent of the people could read and write. But instead of investing in education, Díaz steered his nation relentlessly toward industrialization. Public schools for the masses would simply have to wait.

General Porfirio Díaz

Under the president's rule, Mexico finally joined the industrial age. During his time in office, more than 9,000 miles of railroad tracks were laid down. The output of mines increased threefold, and the value of goods Mexico shipped abroad registered a fivefold gain. New laws, backed by Díaz, encouraged the growth of huge plantations, which produced sugar, coffee, tobacco, cotton, and rubber. Steel plants opened in Nuevo León and textile factories operated in Veracruz.

Employing ironfisted policies, Díaz subdued the highway bandits who had for decades terrorized travelers in Mexico and disrupted the national economy. The president accomplished this miracle by turning the toughest bandit gangs into policemen. Supplied with smart uniforms, silver badges, and menacing-looking broad-brimmed hats, the onetime highway pirates became the famed *rurales* (rural police). Using methods learned through a lifetime of banditry, the rurales gave Mexico the safest roads on earth. By law the rurales were forbidden to execute prisoners, but they were allowed to shoot suspects who they claimed were fleeing custody. During the Díaz administration, some 10,000 men and women were reported "killed while attempting to escape."

Nine out of ten Mexicans lived in farming communities during the Díaz era. The most explosive problem facing the president was landownership, an issue as old as Mexico itself. Under Spain, farmland was divided mostly into *ejidos* owned by Indians and *haciendas* owned by Europeans. Ejidos were tracts of land that were either worked by all of the people of the village or were subdivided into tiny plots and assigned to individual farmers. Haciendas were sprawling farms or ranches owned by one family. A single hacienda often spread over 10,000 acres and employed more than 100 field hands.

Díaz believed that haciendas were more efficient than ejidos, and he allowed wealthy land barons to strip millions of acres from Indian villages. To take over ejido land, hacienda owners twisted the intent of an 1856 law that was designed to break up large estates owned by the Catholic church. Indian villages fought the haciendas in court but won few cases in a system where judges owed their jobs to the whims of Porfirio Díaz.

Díaz's policies gave Mexico armies of landless people along with some of the largest privately owned farms on earth. The Terrazas family in the state of Chihuahua owned more than seven million acres. The Cedros clan of Zacatecas lived on a hacienda that sprawled over almost four million acres. Foreigners frequently bought land that the government had taken from Indians. The American newspaper tycoon and cattle breeder William Randolph Hearst owned a ranch in northern Mexico that was said to be the size of both Maryland and Delaware combined. By contrast, the numbers of landless poor increased every year. In 1895, 20 percent of the Mexican people owned at least a small plot of land or a share in an ejido; in 1910 only 2 percent claimed to be landowners.

The expropriation of Indian land set in motion protests and shooting wars. Following Díaz's orders, the rurales and the army crushed every attempt at rebellion. In the state of Hidalgo, the rurales buried Indian protesters

A group of rurales, *the former bandits used by Díaz to patrol the countryside*

neck-deep in the ground and then galloped over their heads with horses. To protect their land, the Yaqui Indians of Sonora barricaded themselves in the hills, and a war fought with barbaric cruelty began. Cash bounties were

awarded to anyone bringing in a Yaqui ear or hand. Finally the Yaquis were starved out of their mountain hideouts. The governor of Sonora, Ramón Corral—who later became Díaz's vice president—ordered all Yaqui leaders shot.

A new class of landless farmers rose in rural Mexico. These farmers without farms were exploited by large plantation owners who ran what amounted to slave camps. One such camp was a tobacco plantation called Valle Nacional in the state of Oaxaca. There plantation owners induced jobless farmers to sign contracts promising their labor in the tobacco fields for at least a year. The illiterate farmer who put his customary *X* on the contract had no way of knowing he was signing into a form of slavery. The plantation owners deducted for food, clothing, housing, and other expenses, including "legal fees." At the end of the month, the field-worker was given a statement declaring his debt instead of the wages he expected.

At least 15,000 new workers were herded into the Valle Nacional each year. About 10 percent of the laborers were prisoners who had committed petty crimes or were jailed as political troublemakers. Politicians sold the convicts to plantation owners for $45 a head. In the Valle Nacional the workers were forced to pick tobacco under the blistering sun, sleep amid swarms of mosquitoes, and live on a starvation diet. Escape through the jungles and mountains that ringed the valley was impossible. A worker who failed to please his bosses was tied to the whipping post and lashed. The American writer John Kenneth Turner interviewed a Valle Nacional plantation owner who claimed, "By the sixth or seventh month they [the workers] begin to die off like flies at the first winter frost....The cheapest thing to do is to let them die; there are plenty more where they came from."

Hacienda hired hands fared little better than the con-

An engraving depicts the horrible treatment endured by field workers at the hands of wealthy landowners.

tract laborers. Many field-workers had recently lost titles to their lands to the ever-expanding haciendas. Often they tilled the same soil that had been owned by their families for generations. As was true with the contract laborers, the hacienda workers ran up debts that could not be repaid in a lifetime. Debts were passed from father to son so that babies were born owing the hacienda their labor. Escaping the hacienda was a criminal offense since it meant running out on debt payments. Although they were free Mexican citizens, the workers commonly were tied up and whipped by the hacienda owners for a multitude of offenses. Stealing even the smallest item of hacienda-owned property was punishable by 200 lashes—in most cases this was a death penalty.

Certainly Díaz was aware of the conditions in rural Mexico. Journalists had written dozens of reports about the horrors of the labor camps. It was said that Díaz wept upon hearing of one Indian village losing its ejido land to the hacienda. But the president was determined to march Mexico into a new age of industrial and agricultural efficiency. Ejidos were an old-fashioned institution.

The policies of the president took a new twist in 1900 when Díaz fell under the spell of a small group of businessmen called the *científicos* (scientists). Headed by Finance Minister José Limantour, the científicos believed the problems of government and the national economy could be solved by the proper application of scientific principles. For example, the científicos concluded that Mexico needed foreign investment if it was to continue on the road toward industrial development. Foreign investors sought low wages, low taxes, no labor unrest, and subsidies from the government. The científicos assured foreign interests they would find all of these blessings in Mexico.

The científicos, all of whom were whites whose families had arrived since independence, believed Indians and mestizos were suitable for manual labor only. Therefore, they allowed American and European companies to bring in all the skilled personnel they wished. The Indians and mestizos, who comprised 90 percent of the population of Mexico in 1910, were relegated to only the lowliest jobs.

Until the rise of the científicos, Díaz had ruled dictatorially, but he ruled like a Mexican. His cabinet ministers and the businessmen he favored included many mestizos and some Indians. Yet Díaz—who was himself of mostly Indian blood—acceded to the white supremacist, proforeign policies of the científicos. Soon American companies ran Mexico's railroads and owned three-quarters of its mines and more than half of its oil fields. American commitment to Mexico grew to $1 billion, even more than Mexican businesses had invested in their country. Foreign firms came to own one-third of the Mexican economy. British interests acquired gold and silver mines. The French operated the textile mills. Spaniards owned tobacco and coffee plantations. A popular saying uttered by Mexicans throughout the country went, "Mexico, mother to foreigners; stepmother to Mexicans."

The arrival of foreign businesses provided jobs but did little to improve the lives of Mexican workers. In fact, the sudden influx of foreign money raised the prices of corn and other necessities. But, as the científicos had promised, Mexican workers' wages remained low. Labor unions were broken up by local police or by the army. In terms of the price of corn, the average Mexican laborer earned less in 1910 than in 1810. Human labor became so cheap that it cost more per day to rent a mule than it did to hire a man.

In office Díaz grew graceful and respected with age. After his wife died, he married the 18-year-old daughter of a wealthy Mexico City businessman. Cultured and dignified, she taught the president certain niceties, such as the proper knife and fork to use with each course served at a formal dinner. The president's young wife also busied herself with civic projects such as planting trees in Mexico City's broad boulevards.

Because of Mexico's industrial progress, leaders in world capitals heaped praise upon Porfirio Díaz. In many respects the praise was justified. He was the only government figure since independence strong enough to end the barracks rebellions that had thrown the country into anarchy. He had taken Mexico out of debt, and he brought factories to a once backward land. American president Theodore Roosevelt suggested that Washington could have used an administrator as accomplished as Díaz. An often quoted compliment was made by an American businessman: "That Porfirio Díaz might have brown skin, but he has the soul of a white man."

Chapter 2

The
GATHERING
STORM

......

A Revolution in Mexico is impossible.

—The Mexico City newspaper
El Imparcial *in 1909*

he Paseo de la Reforma is a broad, tree-lined boulevard that cuts through the heart of Mexico City. In 1910 the Reforma was the capital's showcase street. Statues and fountains, most of them erected during the Díaz years, decorated the boulevard. At nearby Alameda Park construction workers were building the Grand Opera House, made of Italian marble and a pet project of Díaz's wife. On other downtown streets automobiles chugged alongside brightly polished horse-drawn carriages. Electric streetcars carried shoppers and office workers. People walking past the display windows of department stores wore the latest suits and dresses from Paris and London. Europeans visiting the capital hailed it as "the Paris of the New World."

But if a foreign tourist stood on the sprawling central plaza called the Zócalo and took a brisk 45-minute walk in any direction, he or she would encounter a different world. The outskirts of Mexico City were gathering places for hordes of uprooted farmers who had lost their land to the haciendas and had flocked to the city desperately seeking work. The poor lived in shacks made from discarded building material. Shacks holding 300 or more families were jammed into an area the size of a football field. Running water, sewers, and toilets did not exist in the shack towns. Half the babies born in the poor areas died before their first birthday. Boys and girls who survived never saw the inside of a classroom. The científicos claimed the Mexican budget could not afford to fund schools for the poor.

Twice a day the aging Porfirio Díaz took a one-mile coach ride from his mansion on the Paseo de la Reforma to the National Palace at the Zócalo. Police were especially diligent to clear the streets of beggars during the hours of the president's daily rides. Thanks to the influence of his young wife, Díaz wore only the most tasteful suits, impeccably tailored. His gray handlebar mustache was barbered every morning. He had grown to enjoy parties and balls, especially those hosted by the foreign community. His 80th birthday party was paid for by the state treasury and cost 20 million pesos—twice what the government spent that year on public schools.

Except for a four-year period in the 1880s, Díaz held office for 34 years. Most observers assumed the presidency was his till death. But in 1908 Díaz granted an interview to the American newsman James Creelman and said, "No matter what my friends and supporters say, I retire when my presidential term of office ends [in 1910], and I shall not serve again....I welcome an opposition party in the Mexican Republic. If it appears I will regard it as a blessing, not an evil."

The interview created a sensation. Never before had Díaz indicated he would step down, and not once had he hinted he would tolerate an opposing political party. In the previous two elections, the only person to dare run against Díaz was a lunatic who roamed the streets of Mexico City warning of the coming of tidal waves and adding, as an afterthought, that he was a candidate for president.

By 1910, however, Díaz acted as if the Creelman interview had never taken place. He announced he would be a candidate for reelection and he suppressed rival parties with his customary harshness. Perhaps when he granted the interview he was musing about retirement and then simply changed his mind. Or perhaps he was telling an American reporter what he thought an American audience wanted to hear. Nevertheless, the interview excited the hopes of intellectuals, labor leaders, and journalists who had long ago tired of Díaz's dictatorial rule. These dissidents were willing to support anyone bold enough to stand up to the president. In the northern state of Coahuila, they found their candidate.

Francisco Madero came from an old hacienda-owning family. He was one of the wealthiest men in Mexico. Early in the Díaz administration, his grandfather was a state governor and an ally of the president. Despite his family's wealth and influence, Madero was genuinely concerned with the plight of the poor. From his own pocket he paid for the education of his farm workers' children. He often fed peasant children at the huge dining room table in his hacienda manor house.

Thin, balding, and standing only five feet two inches tall, Madero looked more like a kindly schoolteacher than a political leader. His voice was squeaky, almost birdlike. Many of his personal habits were unusual for the period. In an age when most wealthy men drank brandy and puffed cigars, Madero refused to touch alcohol or tobacco. He was also a strict vegetarian. He practiced a spiritual form of religion, and in times of great personal despair claimed he was able to speak with the soul of his dead brother.

For years Madero had taken a scholarly interest in politics. In 1908 he wrote a book urging free elections in Mexico. With anti-Díaz sentiment on the rise, the book was well received. Madero soon had a small but loyal following among the middle class.

At first Díaz refused to take his opposition seriously. He met with Madero but later told jokes about this vegetarian dreamer whom he called "a little bird." Then, in early 1910, Madero's campaign gained momentum. Crowds swelled as he crisscrossed the country making speeches. His audience grew to include not only the intellectuals and the middle class but also debt-ridden farm

Francisco Madero (seated) with his secretary

workers. Some of those farm workers (campesinos) had backs scarred by the hacienda whip.

Díaz, alarmed by Madero's sudden popularity, reacted in a predictable manner. He had Madero thrown in jail on trumped-up charges.

Election day, June 21, 1910, was ordinary. Díaz won by a huge majority. Earlier the only suspense had been over whom Díaz would choose as his vice president. Insiders speculated it would be José Limantour, the leading científico. Díaz surprised the experts by picking Ramón Corral, who recently had earned a fortune selling the defeated Yaqui people into slavery in the labor camps. Corral was one of the most hated men in Mexico, and many observers believed Díaz chose him as a form of life insurance. Only a fool would assassinate Díaz with Corral next in line to be president.

In Mexico City the great celebration of September 16 began. On that date 100 years earlier, Miguel Hidalgo, a gentle and bookish priest in the town of Dolores, rang the church bell to summon his Indian parishioners to mass. In the churchyard the priest issued the renowned *Grito de Dolores* (cry of Dolores). With that one fiery speech, the Mexican War of Independence was launched.

The Paseo de la Reforma served as the parade ground to honor the first famous *Grito*. Never had the boulevard looked so resplendent as a parade stretching for miles wound by. A half million Mexican citizens crowded the sidewalks to watch. Wildly they cheered the folk dancers and the floats that depicted Mexican history back to Aztec times. But a strange, almost eerie hush overcame the spectators when the open car bearing their president drove past. An American reporter wrote, "Porfirio Díaz, brilliant with royal decorations...swept by without applause."

After the independence celebrations, Díaz released Madero from jail but forbade him from traveling beyond the city limits of San Luis Potosí in northern Mexico. His time spent in jail had jarred Madero's thinking. Throughout his life he had shunned violence. But clearly Porfirio Díaz would accept no peaceful, democratic change in Mexico. Madero was now convinced that only armed rebellion could topple Díaz from power. He prayed the revolution would be short and the bloodshed minimal.

Madero's supporters secretly ushered him across the border to Laredo, Texas. From Texas he issued the Plan of San Luis Potosí, a course of action he conceived while sitting in his prison cell. This was the first of many "plans" devised by revolutionary figures and designed to steer Mexico into a new era of prosperity. The Plan of San Luis Potosí declared the Díaz election illegal and urged Mexicans to take up arms on November 20, 1910, to demand the president step down from office. November 20 came and went. Except for a minor clash in the city of Puebla, no mass uprising broke out. Madero lacked a strong enough following to produce a revolution on demand.

But resistance movements had sprung up in the northern and southern parts of Mexico. The two totally unconnected rebellions that broke out in 1910 were antirich rather than pro-Madero. They were, however, the opening breezes of the great storm about to strike Mexico.

In the rugged northern state of Chihuahua, a cattle rustler and bandit chief named Pancho Villa began a series of devastating raids on wealthy cattle ranches. Villa's horse soldiers were made up of landless Indians and underpaid mestizo miners, all of whom hated the rich. To finance his operations, Villa rustled cattle and used the proceeds to buy guns.

To the south, in the state of Morelos, a farm workers' revolt began under the leadership of Emiliano Zapata. The campesinos of Morelos sought to reclaim the land that was theirs before the expansion of the haciendas. Few of the campesinos could read or write, but all could ride and shoot. Zapata's men stormed haciendas, stole cattle and horses, and melted into the night.

Initially the movements led by Villa and Zapata appeared to be minor upheavals that would soon die out. But instead of ebbing, the rebellions grew in armed force and military spirit. A new, almost unthinkable word now roared through the countryside—revolution, revolution, Revolution!

The first warriors of the Mexican Revolution identified closely with their leaders. Thus Villa's men called themselves the Villistas, while the soldiers of Zapata were known as the Zapatistas. The practice of naming troops after their commanders continued in the later years, when

Pancho Villa leads the Villistas in a maneuver across the Mexican countryside.

the Mexican Revolution became more a conflict of personalities than a battle of ideals.

From Mexico City, Díaz sent armies to Morelos and to the north with orders to snuff out the rebellions. The army units had little success against the hit-and-run Villistas and Zapatistas, who knew every twist and bend in the country roads. In Morelos the Zapatistas captured

General Emiliano Zapata

plantation land and small villages and defended them against the federal armies. The governor of Morelos, who was chased out of the state by the Zapatistas, echoed the growing fear of Mexico's establishment when he told a friend, "These are difficult times....The peasant is now the master."

In the north the Villistas captured the important railway center of the city of Chihuahua. The victory in that city allowed Madero to recross the border and enter Mexico. At Chihuahua, Madero the idealist met Villa the outlaw for the first time. It was the kind of meeting that could take place only under the pressure of war, when strange bedfellows are thrown together. Madero, a white, was a powerful hacienda owner. Villa, a mestizo, was the son of a lowly hacienda worker.

Despite their conflicting backgrounds, the two men developed a friendship based on mutual respect. Villa looked upon Madero as a vital political and intellectual leader of the revolution that was brewing in the land. Madero recognized Villa as a gifted military commander and chose to ignore the stories that he heard about the man's cruel, often murderous moods. However, Madero quickly learned he could not control the bandit chief. He ordered Villa to stay put at Chihuahua, but the outlaw brazenly ignored the order and marched north to even greater plunder.

At the border city of Ciudad Juárez, a bloody house-to-house battle broke out between the Villistas and the federal army defenders. The Villistas were armed with rifles that were relics of past wars. One of their artillery pieces was a 70-year-old cannon that had been stolen from the courthouse lawn in El Paso, Texas. Despite their primitive weapons, Villa and his men displayed a reckless brand of courage and battlefield initiative that would become their signature in the combat to come. When the Villistas found the narrow streets barricaded by federal troops, they dynamited buildings to clear a path for their advance. The city of Ciudad Juárez lies across the Rio Grande from El Paso, Texas. During the height of the fighting, thousands of Americans gathered on rooftops to watch. Several onlookers were wounded by stray bullets. On May 10, 1911, the federal commander of Ciudad Juárez surrendered. Villa gave orders to execute the commander, but at the last minute Madero saved the man's life by escorting him across the border into Texas.

The fall of Ciudad Juárez was decisive. From that city Madero and Villa could supply their forces with modern guns bought in the United States. The Ciudad Juárez victory also ignited uprisings in dozens of smaller villages and hamlets. Soon the great roar of revolution reached the palace doors at Mexico City.

In his mansion on the Paseo de la Reforma, President Díaz bent over maps spread on his favorite billiard table. Furiously he telegraphed orders to the fighting fronts. Now and then he raged about his officers' inability to put down a few revolutionary bandits. At one point the 81-

year-old president told his aides he would personally take the field to direct the troops.

While Díaz fussed over the military situation, the day-to-day functions of government fell to José Limantour, the leading científico. Limantour was a realist who shunned military adventures. With Madero and Villa commanding the north and the rampaging Zapatistas tearing up the state of Morelos in the south, the government's position seemed hopeless. Adding to the government's peril were the angry crowds that gathered every evening on the Zócalo below the National Palace. From his office window Limantour heard their menacing chants: "Death to Díaz. Death to the científicos. Death to Díaz!"

Limantour sent an emissary to Madero asking for terms of peace. Madero and the Limantour representative met in the countryside near Ciudad Juárez on the night of May 21, 1911. On a folding table illuminated by car headlights, the two parties signed an agreement. Díaz and Limantour would resign. Vice President Corral was no longer a factor, because he had escaped into exile at the first sign of trouble. Francisco León de la Barra, the Mexican ambassador to the United States, was to serve as interim president until new elections could be held. The favorite candidate in such elections was clearly Francisco Madero.

News of the agreement electrified Mexico City. Crowds gathered at the Zócalo and in front of the president's mansion. The people banged on oilcans and yelled for Díaz's immediate resignation. A group of young men broke into a chant that had grown popular with the city's labor unions:

> Little work, lots of *dinero* (money)
> Beans for all—*Viva Madero!*

Tragedy struck at the Zócalo when panic-stricken troops fired into the mob. The demonstrators fled and a sudden rain drenched the plaza. Onlookers peering out of windows counted 200 corpses strewn about the Zócalo, their blood running in rain-driven rivulets.

Just before sunrise on May 26, President Díaz—now clearly showing his age—was helped into a limousine. At his side was his young wife. The two were rushed to the railway station, where they boarded a train for the port city of Veracruz. There a ship took them to exile in France. Díaz died in Paris four years later. Before he left the country he had ruled for more than a third of a century, he told a reporter, "They [the revolutionaries] have unleashed dangers they will not be able to control."

A triumphant Francisco Madero entered Mexico City in early June 1911. Joyous crowds shouting, *"Viva Madero!"* and *"Viva la Revolución!"* filled the streets. The overwhelming majority of the people had never seen the little politician or heard him speak. Still, they hailed Madero as a saint delivered to save their nation. But an ominous note dampened the festivities. Almost the moment Madero stepped off the train, a sharp earthquake rocked the capital. The quake sent thousands of terrorized residents streaming into the streets. For many people, especially the Indians, the earthquake held a mystic significance. It was a message from the gods saying the terrible winds sweeping Mexico would not diminish. In fact, the winds of war would become a hurricane.

Chapter 3

MADERO

∎ ∎ ∎ ∎ ∎

**It is true my government has not achieved
peace. But the rights, liberties, and
guarantees we are winning in all sectors
of the nation are worth more than peace.**

—Francisco Madero

n early 1911 Francisco Madero was the most
popular man in Mexico. Wherever he traveled,
he was greeted by excited crowds, brass bands,
and children strewing flowers at his feet. If he wished,
Madero could simply have taken over the office of president without waiting for elections to be held. But Madero
was true to his word. He had agreed to let the interim
government run the country until October, when organized elections were scheduled. As a champion of democracy, he would under no circumstances become president
until he was legitimately elected to that office.

A tense period passed as Mexicans waited for the elections. The nation was still in a state of revolution, and
armed peasant bands remained at the ready in the coun-

Madero's popularity is displayed in this mural showing people cheering him.

tryside. The interim president, Francisco León de la Barra, ordered the rebel armies to lay down their rifles, but his directions were ignored. In the north, Pancho Villa remained aligned with Madero. To show his support for the incoming president, Villa curtailed the activities of his army. The Revolution, which had been a fire, simmered as the diminutive politician Madero campaigned for votes.

Elections took place as planned in October. Madero was swept into office, winning more than 90 percent of the votes cast. He had chosen José María Pino Suárez, a journalist from the state of Yucatán, to be his vice president. Madero and Pino Suárez took their oaths of office on November 6, 1911. At last the Mexican people enjoyed a freely elected president and vice president.

But Madero inherited a nation he was unable to govern. In the countryside the campesinos demanded land that the hacienda owners refused to relinquish. In the cities laborers clamored for a living wage, while profit-minded businessmen ignored their requests.

To the burning demands for land and bread, Madero offered only philosophy. As president he believed his one overriding mission was to make Mexico a democratic country. Once democracy was fully established, he reasoned, the nation's other problems would be settled by mutual agreements reached with all parties. He ignored the grim facts that most Mexicans were poorly fed, ill-clothed, and slept in mud hovels. The president once told a reporter, "The Mexican people are not asking me for bread, they are asking me for liberty."

In office, Madero talked about reforms such as land redistribution, but his talk rarely translated into action. For example, he turned the question of land redistribution over to a committee made up of congressmen. The committee never issued a significant report on the problem. Yet by simply talking about rights for workers and land for peasants, Madero stepped on powerful toes. Hacienda owners, mine owners, and Mexico City and foreign businessmen began to brand him as a dangerous radical. The president was caught in a cross fire between the political right and the political left. In just a matter of months, the once widely popular Madero lost much of his support.

The Mexico City press took particular delight in bashing the president. The liberal newspapers complained that he was sitting on his hands on the land issue, while the conservative press denounced him as being antibusiness. The attacks in the newspapers were especially ironic because during the Díaz years the press was closely censored. Madero, believing a free press was a cornerstone of democracy, lifted the censorship. As the president's popularity sagged, the newly liberated newspapers continued their campaign against his government. One cartoonist portrayed Madero as a figure flattened on the pavement, and at the figure's head was a steamroller labeled PUBLIC OPINION. The president's brother, Gustavo Madero, who held a high cabinet position, accused the newspapers of "biting the hand that removed the muzzle."

The explosive issue of land ownership simply would not disappear in a swell of democratic energy as the president hoped it would. The status of hacienda workers remained the same under Madero as it was under Díaz. The workers were deeply in debt and they often tilled the same fields that were owned by their fathers and grandfathers before the Díaz government spurred the expansion of haciendas.

Champion of the landless campesinos was Emiliano Zapata. He refused to listen to Madero's argument that democracy would cure all the nation's ills. To Zapata the president's democratic idealism was a jumble of empty words. The peasant leader's background dictated to him that landownership was as important to the Mexican people as were breath and blood.

Emiliano Zapata was born in 1879 in the village of Anenecuilco, located in the heart of Morelos. He was of mostly Indian blood, with skin as brown as the earth of his native land. He came from a poor but respected family in the village of 400 people. When Emiliano was only nine years old, he first witnessed the power exercised by a large landholder. A hacienda owner who had close ties with the state government leveled an entire neighborhood near Anenecuilco in order to create grazing land for his horses. Emiliano found his father weeping over the ruins of the neighborhood chapel.

"Why don't you fight the hacienda owner?" Emiliano asked.

"The owner is too strong," his father answered.

The nine-year-old future revolutionary leader shook his head in mystification. He failed entirely to understand why his father and the other village men cowered under hacienda authority.

As a youth, Zapata was handsome, athletic, and the best horseman the local people had ever seen. He worked on ranches and for a while held a job as a trick rider for a rodeo show. His work took him to Mexico City, a place his neighbors thought was a foreign world as far away as the face of the moon. Always Zapata returned to the village, and always he saw the hacienda's property grow while the village ejido shrank. By the time Zapata was in his 20s, the local campesinos had been reduced to share-croppers who farmed parcels of land "rented" to them by the hacienda owners.

In 1909 the villagers chose Zapata to go to the governor of Morelos and ask his help to reclaim the lands taken from them by the hacienda owner. The governor sent Zapata home, refusing even to talk to him. In fact, just the mere request the villagers made to the governor infuriated the hacienda owner so greatly he forbade the campesinos from farming even as sharecroppers. In a letter the owner told the villagers, "If the people of Anenecuilco want to plant corn, let them plant it in a flowerpot, because not even on the hillsides are they going to have the use of my land."

After this incident, Zapata concluded that landowners in Morelos would never peacefully surrender their stolen ejido properties. If the campesinos wanted their ejidos back, they would have to retake them with guns, clubs, machetes, or whatever other weapons they could gather. Emiliano Zapata became a revolutionary, and he was destined to be the most respected revolutionary leader in Mexico.

Under Zapata's leadership the great hacienda war began in Morelos. His method of battle was simple: Attack haciendas and make off with horses, rifles, and whatever cash his men could find. In combat he was bold and inventive. Early in the campaign he commandeered a train that ran on a special track built to connect the large haciendas. Loading his men aboard the train, he sent it crashing full speed through a hacienda gate. The surprised defenders surrendered the hacienda.

The government, first under Díaz and then under the interim president León de la Barra, sent armies into the south to crush the Zapatista rebellion. When the troops could not flush the Zapatistas out of the mountain region, they resorted to terror tactics. Suspected Zapata supporters were not only hanged, they were hanged over a smoldering fire so they suffered the triple agonies of smoke in their lungs, fire at their feet, and rope around their necks. One general, Juvencio Robles, boasted, "If they [the Zapatistas] resist me, I shall hang them like earrings to the trees."

Despite the cruelties imposed by government soldiers, the hacienda war raged on. When Zapata took over a hacienda, he practiced his own form of land redistribution. He gave away portions of land to the local people and told them to farm it while at the same time protecting it from government soldiers. Often Zapata's male and

Hanged men served as a grim reminder of the brutality that marked much of the Mexican Revolution.

female supporters tilled the soil with rifles slung around their shoulders. As the Zapata movement grew, his peasant army took over scores of haciendas as well as several small cities.

On two occasions, before he became president, Madero met with Zapata. Madero, a man of peace, was horrified by the brutality of the hacienda war. He agreed the large haciendas should be split up, but he insisted the hacienda owners be paid for the land they would lose. Therefore, land reform would have to wait until the Mexican treasury had sufficient money. Zapata scoffed at the need to pay the hacienda owners. He suspected the payment scheme was a delaying tactic used by Madero. He reminded Madero that the haciendas had stolen land from village ejidos, and no one had paid the villagers.

By the time Madero took his oath of office, Zapata had publicly denounced him as an enemy of the Revolution. Then, on November 27, 1911, Zapata made a grand gesture that will be remembered forever in the pages of Mexican history. At the tiny town of Ayala in Morelos, a ragtag band played the Mexican national anthem. Emiliano Zapata, with the flag of Mexico draped around him, emerged from an adobe hut. There he revealed the Plan of Ayala, his program for land reform: "The land, forests, and water which have been usurped...through tyranny and venal justice, will be restored immediately to the villages or citizens who have corresponding titles to them....They [the villagers] shall maintain such lands at all costs with their arms."

In Mexico City, President Madero was unable to stop the rampaging Zapatistas to the south. Because he could not put an end to the hacienda war, the Mexico City press branded him a coward. One writer claimed his vegetarian diet somehow made the president unmanly and therefore incapable of commanding the nation. Other editorial writers, forgetting they were once strictly censored, longed for the stability of the Díaz era. A popular Mexico City daily asked, "What remains for us of the order, peace, prosperity, and respect abroad which Mexico enjoyed under the government of General Díaz?"

Adding to Madero's problems was the meddlesome American ambassador to Mexico, Henry Lane Wilson. Like many Mexican businessmen, Wilson believed Madero to be a dangerous radical. The ambassador was particularly enraged when Madero levied a tax on oil companies in order to fund public education in Mexico. At the time American firms owned huge oil fields throughout the nation. Wilson sent prejudiced and often erroneous reports to President William Howard Taft in Washington, D.C. The reports portrayed Mexico as being in a state of turmoil, even though revolutionary warfare was largely confined to the south. In one report Wilson said, "There is no peace, there is no order, the rabble is rising, the man [Madero] is mad."

With Madero's popularity waning and his list of ene-mies growing, it was not long before ambitious men sought to overthrow him and seize the presidency. The most dangerous of these would-be presidents was Pascual Orozco, a onetime ally of Pancho Villa. Orozco was an unsmiling man who bore a sinister resemblance to a typical villain in a Western movie. In March 1912 Orozco began a rebellion against the government of Francisco Madero. The rebel leader had a well-equipped army of 6,000 men. His rifles and horses were supplied largely by the Terrazas and Creel families of northern Mexico. The two families were powerful landowners who feared that someday Madero would implement his talked-about plans for land reform.

Pascual Orozco hoped to march his army south to Mexico City, gathering followers as he traveled. The rebellion had a bloody beginning in the northern state of Chihuahua. Orozco's men loaded a train with dynamite and sent it screaming head-on into another train carrying federal troops. Most of the government soldiers riding the train were blown to bits. The few survivors were too dazed to fight back against Orozco's soldiers.

To put down the Orozco rebellion, President Madero turned to General Victoriano Huerta. This choice proved to be the president's greatest mistake. Huerta was a brutal but effective officer. During the Díaz years, he had crushed many revolts among the Indians. His fellow officers knew Huerta as a hard drinker, a drug user, and a corrupt soldier who routinely pocketed army funds.

President Madero detested war, and he had deep mis-

General Victoriano Huerta

givings about the character of General Huerta. Yet the president believed he had no choice but to defeat the Orozco rebellion by force of arms. He authorized Huerta to lead a large army and gave him one million pesos from the national treasury. After two battles in northern Mexico, Huerta routed Orozco's troops. Pascual Orozco was forced to flee across the border and take exile in Texas. The campaign was relatively easy, and afterward President Madero asked Huerta how much money remained of the million pesos he had given him. Huerta said he had spent all the money. An angry Madero demanded to see his records. Huerta said defiantly, "I am a soldier, not a book-keeper."

Chapter 4

The
TEN
TRAGIC
DAYS

......

It was a spectacle difficult to forget. When the dead were burned...they writhed as if trying to sit up.

—A resident of Mexico City remembering the ghastly bonfires made up of dead bodies

adero's Mexico teemed with generals. Leaders of even the tiniest guerrilla bands called themselves generals and sought the prestige and riches associated with that rank. From this vast pool of generals came power-hungry men eager to depose Madero and seize the presidency. One ambitious self-proclaimed general was Felix Díaz, nephew of the ex-dictator Porfirio Díaz. Felix Díaz enjoyed the support of landowners and businessmen who were eager to return to the comforts they enjoyed under the regime of his famous uncle. A group of wealthy men gave Felix Díaz a large sum of money and asked him to bring back the good old days.

At two in the morning of February 9, 1913, a column of soldiers equipped with horse-drawn cannons wound their way along a lonely street that cut through Mexico City's lovely Chapultepec Park. The soldiers marched quietly, but they created enough of a racket to alert a security guard. The guard notified his superior. Word of the unusual troop movement soon reached Gustavo Madero, the president's brother.

Gustavo Madero was the muscle behind the presidency. Unlike his brother, Gustavo believed in dealing out harsh punishments to upstart generals. And unlike his brother, he was quick to recognize treachery. As soon as he was told of troops on the march, Gustavo hurried to the National Palace, which stood at the Zócalo, the city's venerable central plaza.

The soldiers advancing in the night were part of a coup d'état hatched by General Felix Díaz and his supporters. Díaz was confident the coup d'état would be an easy operation because the guard unit at the National Palace was in on the conspiracy and would offer no resistance. But Díaz did not know that Gustavo Madero had arrived at the National Palace hours earlier and replaced the disloyal guards with his own men.

It was a brilliant Sunday morning when the column of rebel troops approached Zócalo. The plaza was crowded with churchgoers headed for Mass at the towering cathedral that rose on the Zócalo's north side. Feeling a surge of confidence, the men crossed the plaza to the National Palace, the seat of presidential authority.

Suddenly a shot pierced the morning calm. Next a

crescendo of rifle fire rang out. Machine guns appeared on the roof of the National Palace and sprayed the Zócalo. The officer leading the rebels fell off his horse, dead with a bullet in his face. After ten terrifying minutes the gunfire diminished and the troops fled. The plaza was covered with corpses. Blood-soaked wounded people cried out in pain. Most of the dead and wounded were parishioners on their way to Mass.

What followed is known in Mexican history as the *Decena Trágica,* the Ten Tragic Days. It was a nightmare period when a pitched ten-day battle was fought in the heart of the city crowded with some one million people. The Mexican capital had not experienced such bloodshed since the Spaniards conquered the Aztecs here 400 years earlier.

Felix Díaz and the rebel soldiers retreated about a mile away from the Zócalo to a thick-walled building called the *Ciudadela,* the Citadel. There they set up artillery and began to bombard the Zócalo area. Within minutes several downtown buildings crumbled under the impact of shells. A dozen fires broke out. Terrified civilians ran screaming through the streets.

In the National Palace, President Madero made a strange, inexplicable decision. He gave command of the city to General Victoriano Huerta and told him to crush the Felix Díaz uprising. General Huerta eagerly accepted the assignment. He lined the Zócalo with big guns and ordered his men to fire toward the Citadel. A thundering artillery duel began in the heart of the crowded city.

Days followed hellish nights on the urban battlefield. Entire neighborhoods were leveled. Families slept under mattresses to ward off shell splinters. Women who were forced to venture into the streets to seek food held up white sheets tied to brooms. Their flags of innocence did them little good, as the mindless cannonading raged on. Bodies littered the streets.

But even inexperienced soldiers observing this bloody scene asked the question, "What good is all the cannon fire?" Gunners at the Zócalo were unable to hit the Citadel because too many tall buildings stood in their line of fire. Artillerymen at the Citadel faced the same obstacles. Yet the two generals—especially General Huerta—continued the bombardments even though they knew they were only killing civilians huddling in their homes.

Unknown to the suffering civilians, General Huerta looked upon this battle as a grand opportunity for him to become president. He despised Madero and had long planned to overthrow him. The general hoped the murderous cannonading would make the people of Mexico City demand peace at any price. If Madero was forced to step down from office, Huerta could then assume the presidency and declare peace to a relieved city. The general believed he could strike a deal with Felix Díaz. All he needed was a mediator, a go-between, to arrange a meeting between General Díaz and himself. Huerta found that mediator in American ambassador Henry Lane Wilson.

Wilson, a corporate lawyer from Indiana, was an advocate of "dollar diplomacy"—a belief that an American diplomat's primary mission was to advance the cause of American businesses operating abroad. In Mexico, American companies had for years made enormous profits because they employed cheap labor and paid virtually no taxes. Then Madero became president. While he did little to change the privileges American companies enjoyed, he nonetheless spoke of a future Mexico where large companies paid taxes and where labor unions had the right to organize. To Ambassador Wilson, such talk bordered on communism. Madero had to go.

Ambassador Wilson helped to arrange a series of secret meetings between Huerta and Felix Díaz. Gustavo Madero got wind of these meetings and demanded an explanation from General Huerta. Huerta admitted holding secret talks with Díaz but claimed his discussions were an effort to get the rebel leader to surrender. When Gustavo was unconvinced, Huerta ordered a battalion of troops to assault the Citadel in broad daylight. The troops were cut down in a withering cross fire from the Citadel's defenders. Huerta knew he was sending the attackers into certain death, but he was willing to sacrifice them in a farcical demonstration of loyalty to Gustavo Madero.

While Huerta was busy deceiving the president's brother, the cannons rained ever-greater destruction on Mexico City. Stores, hospitals, churches, and apartment buildings crumbled to rubble. Fires blazed out of control.

People huddled in the wreckage of their homes, too terri-fied to step outside. As the shells thundered, Mexico City dwellers ate pet cats and dogs in order to survive. Bodies and parts of bodies lay strewn in the street. Battered resi-dents feared disease would spread because of the decom-posing corpses. During lulls in the shelling, volunteers rushed into the streets, pushed the bodies into piles, doused them with gasoline, and created grisly bonfires.

The Ten Tragic Days lasted from February 9 to Febru-ary 18, 1913. While the capital's residents trembled under a storm of shells, Felix Díaz and Victoriano Huerta con-cluded a secret pact. The agreement was later called the Pact of the Embassy because it had the full blessing of Ambassador Henry Lane Wilson. Under terms of the pact, Huerta agreed to dismiss his guards from the National Palace and allow the Díaz coup d'état to suc-ceed. Then Huerta would proclaim himself acting presi-dent until elections could be held. The elections would be arranged so that Felix Díaz would win the presidency.

On the afternoon of February 18, General Huerta was conveniently absent from the National Palace. He was instead at a hotel safely away from the shelling, having lunch with Gustavo Madero. While they dined, a team of specially trained soldiers rushed into President Madero's office and seized him and Vice President Pino Suárez. The luncheon at the hotel was interrupted by a telephone call. Huerta excused himself to answer it. The caller told him the president was under custody. Huerta reentered the

A satirical engraving depicts U.S Ambassador Henry Lane Wilson playing chess with the figures of Huerta, Madero, and Zapata.

dining room, a pistol in his hand. He announced to Gustavo Madero that he was under arrest.

The shelling that spread terror in Mexico City for ten days ceased at last. Dazed survivors emerged from their shelters to look at the wreckage of their city. Many people fell to their knees and prayed in thanksgiving for the sudden silence. Church bells pealed. Ambassador Wilson sent a telegram to Washington: MEXICO HAS BEEN SAVED. FROM NOW ON WE SHALL HAVE PEACE, PROGRESS, AND PROSPERITY.

The terrible time of the *Decena Trágica* was over. Huerta was in command of Mexico City. Now he had to decide the fate of the previous leaders.

Huerta hated Gustavo Madero even more than he did the president. As soon as the shelling diminished, Huerta turned Gustavo over to a band of Díaz's men in the Citadel. Most of Díaz's followers were bandits, not soldiers. Worse yet, they had become gloriously drunk celebrating their victory. The men beat and kicked Gustavo Madero and gouged him with their bayonets. When he dropped to his knees, pleading for his life, they laughed at him. Finally, mercifully, an officer shot him in the head.

President Madero and Vice President Pino Suárez remained under arrest in Huerta's hands. The president had no idea his brother had been savagely murdered. But the rest of the world learned of Gustavo's death the next day, when Mexico City newspapers carried the story on their front pages. Now it was clear the lives of Madero and Pino Suárez were in grave danger.

Dozens of foreign capitals, including Washington, sent urgent letters to Huerta, imploring him not to harm Madero. A personal appeal came from Pedro Lascuráin, who served as Madero's foreign minister. According to Lascuráin, General Huerta tore off his shirt to expose the Virgin of Guadalupe medal he wore around his neck. The Virgin of Guadalupe is Mexico's patron saint; her image is sacred. Holding the medal near his heart, Huerta swore by the Virgin that he would not harm Madero. Lascuráin was satisfied by this oath.

But Madero's family still feared for his life. Huerta refused to speak with Madero's wife, Sara, so she appeared before Ambassador Wilson. During a long and tearful interview, Sara expressed her dread that Huerta would soon murder her husband. She showed Wilson a letter from Madero's mother, begging the ambassador to help rescue her son. Wilson replied that Madero's fate was in the hands of General Huerta. Any move on his part to influence Huerta's decisions would amount to American intervention in Mexico's internal affairs. Wilson claimed it was not his policy to meddle in Mexico's political matters.

It was near midnight on the night of February 22, 1913, when an officer entered the room where Francisco Madero was being held. The officer said that Madero and the vice president were being transferred to a prison on the outskirts of Mexico City. Madero and Pino Suárez were put into separate cars and driven into the night. At the edge of town, the cars braked to a stop. The doors swung open, and Madero and Pino Suárez were pushed out. An officer shot them both repeatedly in the head. During the assassinations, Huerta was at the American Embassy. He, Ambassador Wilson, and others were celebrating a Washington's Birthday party.

The next morning Huerta announced that Madero and Pino Suárez were shot and killed while attempting to escape custody. Ambassador Wilson sent a telegram to his superiors in Washington, urging them to accept the explanation.

Huerta sits on a throne above the bodies of President Madero and Vice President Suarez in this engraving by Alfredo Zalce.

Chapter 5

HUERTA

. . . . .

A revolution is fought by flesh and blood men, not by saints, and every revolution ends with the creation of a new privileged class.

—A character created by the Mexican novelist Carlos Fuentes

he democratic gains ushered in by Madero were quickly cast aside by Huerta. After taking office, Huerta jailed 110 members of Congress. The press was gagged again. Huerta dismissed judges, replacing them with his handpicked cronies. The elections he promised were never held. Felix Díaz, who now cowered under Huerta's authority, was shipped to Japan on a diplomatic mission. Sham elections did take place, but the vote count was unimportant. Huerta had already declared himself the winner and the new president.

In terms of brutality the Huerta regime was harsher than that of Porfirio Díaz. To prevent a counterrevolution, Huerta had 100 Madero supporters shot. Abraham González, the pro-Madero governor of Chihuahua, was thrown under the wheels of a slow-moving train by

Huerta henchmen. A particularly courageous congressman named Belisario Domínguez delivered a speech
condemning Huerta as a tyrant. During the speech, the
congressman predicted his own assassination because he
dared to criticize the president. Two weeks later
Domínguez's bullet-ridden body was found in a ditch in a
Mexico City suburb.

While Huerta fought with cunning and cruelty to
keep his office, he showed little zest for the day-to-day
work of the presidency. He enjoyed drinking cognac and
smoking marijuana. He preferred barrooms and gambling
houses to the presidential office. His time as president was
characterized by government limousines racing from one
Mexico City saloon to another as harried bureaucrats tried
to find the president to have him sign vital papers.

Despite his deficiencies, Huerta enjoyed powerful supporters. The landowners were kindly disposed toward
him, as was the American business community. The army
was proud that one of their own was president. And he
had the blessings of the Catholic church, an important
force in the nation.

The Mexican Catholic church had a speckled history.
At the time of the Spanish Conquest, the church was a
civilizing influence. The Spanish conquistadores had the
mentality of pirates and enslaved the Indians, killing them
and torturing them at will. Many brave Spanish priests
protected the Native Americans from the abuses of their
countrymen. But shortly after the Conquest, the church

brought the horrors of the Spanish Inquisition to Mexico. During the Inquisition years, men and women accused of being heretics were burned at the stake in the Zócalo and in other public squares.

By the 1850s the church was the nation's largest single landowner. It dominated education and influenced government. President Benito Juárez tried to break the power of the church. A bloody civil war erupted between church supporters and the Juárez movement. The Díaz government reversed the antichurch stand taken by Juárez. Under Díaz the church regained much of its old power and influence.

Madero's election angered church leaders. As president, Madero wanted to reinforce Mexico's 1857 constitution, which had been adopted by Juárez. That constitution called for the separation of church and state, similar to provisions in the American constitution. Huerta, as was true with Díaz before him, ignored the 1857 constitution and allowed the church to regain its old privileges. In return, priests held special masses celebrating Huerta's presidency.

Because of its support of men like Díaz and Huerta, the Catholic church became a villain in the eyes of Mexican revolutionaries. Still, few of the revolutionary leaders proclaimed atheism. Instead they declared that the Catholic church of Mexico had drifted away from God. Thus the Revolution embraced an anticlerical (antichurch rather than antireligion) position. Pancho Villa echoed the views of revolutionaries when he told a writer, "I believe in God, but not religion. They are all frauds, the priests and the nuns. I shall do what I can to take the church out of politics and to open the eyes of the people to the thieving priests."

Despite Huerta's support from the church, Mexico was aflame with revolution. By killing Madero, Huerta had succeeded only in making him a martyr. Even those generals and politicians who thought Madero was an incompetent president now praised him and called upon Mexicans to take up arms to overthrow his murderer. One of the men intent on deposing Huerta was Venustiano Carranza, the governor of the northern state of Coahuila.

Venustiano Carranza was an unlikely revolutionary leader. White-skinned and of European blood, he was born into a family of rich landowners. He enjoyed elegant food and always wore tailored suits. Pancho Villa once complained that Carranza smelled of "damned perfume" instead of sweat and dust, the proper scent of a man. Carranza was a Madero supporter, and he refused to accept Huerta as president after the assassination. Calling his supporters together, he announced still another plan—the Plan of Guadalupe. The plan was simple: It called for the overthrow of Huerta and the restoration of the 1857 constitution. With the spirit of rebellion filling the air, Carranza had little trouble assembling an army. He began to call himself the First Chief of the Revolution.

Northern Mexicans always considered themselves a

breed apart from their countrymen in Mexico City and the south. The north is bleak desert land, the home of Indian tribes and tough, independent ranchers. The desolate region was never truly conquered by the Spaniards, nor was it ruled tightly by Mexico City. A frontier spirit prevailed in the north, breeding men such as Carranza, the First Chief; Pancho Villa, the bandit turned revolutionary; and finally the man who would become the most successful leader of the Revolution—Alvaro Obregón from the state of Sonora.

Obregón was of European descent, but unlike Carranza he had not been born into wealth. As a young man Obregón had worked as a small farmer, a mechanic in a factory, and a schoolteacher. He once invented and patented a farm implement that picked chickpeas mechanically, thus relieving field hands from a backbreaking job. Obregón had lived among the Yaqui Indians in Sonora and witnessed them being robbed of their land during the Díaz dictatorship. A onetime Madero supporter, he became a revolutionary after the assassination. At first his army was made up almost entirely of Yaquis armed only with bows and arrows. Despite their lack of weapons, the Yaquis fought with a desperate fury that struck terror into the hearts of their opponents. Stripped of the land they loved, the Yaqui warriors raced screaming into battle like men who had nothing to lose.

In Mexico City, President Huerta found himself surrounded. To the south raged the hacienda war led by

Emiliano Zapata. In the north Obregón assembled his force of Yaquis, while Pancho Villa gathered an army made up of unemployed mestizo mine workers. In the northwest Carranza built his army around hard-riding cowboys. The armies of the north bought their weapons from willing arms dealers in the United States. They raised money by rustling cattle and holding wealthy landowners for ransom payments.

The northern generals—Villa, Obregón, and Carranza—operated independently of one another. But the three men proclaimed some common goals. They were officially anticlerical, and they called for the ouster of Victoriano Huerta. The leaders of the north also said they wanted to reestablish the constitution of 1857. Thus Carranza, Obregón, and Villa became known as the Constitutionalists. Finally all the armies had a common slogan, which they used to recruit troops and instill bravery. It was a simple saying, but it became the ringing battle cry of the Revolution: "*Tierra y Libertad,* Land and Liberty!"

To counter the strength of his enemies, Huerta mustered an army of his own. He drew his army primarily from the men of Mexico City, one of the few places in the nation where he employed complete control. All males between 15 and 40 were obliged to serve. Huerta sent recruiters to the bullfights, to the saloons, anywhere men might gather. Mexico City men were afraid to walk the streets lest they be abducted by Huerta's officers. Some men ventured outside with babies in their arms, hoping

Some of the young soldiers conscripted by Huerta's forces to fight the rebels

that the presence of an infant would ward off the recruiters. But the tactic failed. The men were grabbed and hurried off to army barracks, leaving distraught mothers to pick up their babies at the police station. Using these strong-arm tactics, Huerta collected a force of 200,000 men, a fourfold increase over his old federal army.

By late 1913 practically everyone in Mexico was swept up in the whirlwind force of revolution. Lawyers, doctors, and college students served in rebel armies alongside barefoot peasants. Some soldiers had clear ideas and burning convictions as to why they wanted to fight: Death to the tyrant Huerta. Down with the rich. Land to the campesinos. Others joined the revolution simply because they were overwhelmed with the excitement of the times. One of Villa's men told an American journalist, "It is good, fighting, you don't have to work in the mines."

Across the border United States government leaders watched the situation in Mexico with growing concern. Shortly after Madero's assassination the ex-college professor Woodrow Wilson was inaugurated as president. Wilson rejected dollar diplomacy. He had become an admirer of Madero and hoped to see a democratic government rise in Mexico. The new president recalled Henry Lane Wilson (no relation) from Mexico, because he suspected the ambassador had given false reports to former president Taft. But although Woodrow Wilson was well-meaning, many Mexicans suspected he was another meddling

United States California, Texas, Arizona, and other territory that had once belonged to Mexico. Now the bully to the north had again invaded Mexican soil. Mexican patriots, even those who despised Huerta, rallied behind him when he denounced the invasion. The American marines occupied Veracruz for seven months. During that time Mexico City mobs broke the windows of American-owned buildings and toppled the statue of George Washington that stood downtown.

Still, the outrage felt by Mexicans over the invasion of Veracruz could not save Huerta's skin. From Zapata's peasant army in the south to the Constitutionalist uprising in the north, the vise was closing. War was a firestorm sweeping over Mexico, driven by a savage wind.

Chapter 6

WAR CONSUMES MEXICO

......

If I am to die tomorrow
Let them kill me today

—From the song "La Valentina,"
which was favored by the Zapatistas

or me the war began when I was born," said Pancho Villa. "God brought me into the world to battle." Few people had reason to doubt the guerrilla leader's statement. As war became a way of life, Villa's army emerged as the most daring and the most feared of the revolutionary bands that ravaged the north.

Pancho Villa was a bandit. He claimed he was forced into that underground profession because of a tragic boyhood. A dark-skinned mestizo, he grew up in the northern state of Durango, where his father was an impoverished sharecropper. He became an outlaw after he shot and killed a wealthy landowner. The landowner, according to a story often told by Villa, had raped Villa's sister. Forced to go on the run, Villa joined a gang of cattle rustlers. To celebrate his membership in the gang, he changed his name from Doroteo Arango (the name given to him at birth) to Francisco (Pancho) Villa. He chose the name Pancho Villa to honor a local bandit chief who had just been killed.

Mexicans distinguished between *bandidos* (bandits) and *ladrónes* (thieves). A ladrón steals from his friends and his neighbors. Ladrónes are scum who deserve to be shot on sight. A bandido, on the other hand, is a bit of a Robin Hood. Bandidos rob from the people who already have far more than they need. The true bandido uses his money to help the poor. During the harsh years of revolutionary fighting, Villa often gave away food supplies to impoverished villagers. However, when he doled out food, he made certain there was a journalist or two present to record the event. Like an American politician, Villa was protective of his image, and he enjoyed promoting his image as a man of the people.

A lifetime of experience as a bandit gave Pancho Villa the skills he needed to wage what he felt was a holy war against Huerta and his army. His first major victory came at the border town of Ciudad Juárez, a city he had captured three years earlier for his hero Madero. At the second battle of Ciudad Juárez, Villa's army was small. Villa knew a cavalry charge against the Juárez garrison would be suicide. So he and his men commandeered a train pulling hopper cars filled with coal. They dumped the coal on the ground and climbed into the cars. Villa used the train as both a Trojan horse and as a modern armored personnel carrier. When the federal troops at Ciudad Juárez saw the engine and the long string of cars approach, they were not alarmed, thinking it was just another coal train. Then, as the train neared the federal army's position, Villa's men popped up, firing their rifles from the protection of the thick-walled iron cars. Ciudad Juárez fell to Villa, and the federals suffered major casualties.

Villa's cavalry charges became the stuff of legends in the north. His horse soldiers were called the *Dorados*, the golden ones, named for their gold-hued uniforms. The Dorados wore broad cartwheel hats and often had bandoleers of ammunition slung crosswise over their chests. Their general, Pancho Villa, led every cavalry charge himself. Villa stood six feet tall and weighed a muscular 200 pounds. On foot he walked with a clumsy gait, stumbling often. But on horseback he displayed the grace of an Olympian. His face was a mask of anger when he led a charge. To him fear was a disease that plagued weaklings. Above the thunder of hoofbeats, his men shouted battle cries: "Viva Pancho Villa!" "Death to the federals!" *"Viva la Revolución!"*

Because they had to cover great distances, the armies of the north traveled on trains. Villa's troop movements resembled mass migrations. Horses rode on cattle cars, artillery on flatcars, soldiers on boxcars, and officers in the caboose. The trains were always overcrowded, and younger soldiers were assigned to sit on the roofs of box-

A train loaded with Villa's troops makes its way across the country.

cars. The federal army also relied on trains to transport its soldiers. Consequently northern Mexico's railroad lines became long, narrow battlefields. Hand-pumped cars or old engines were loaded with dynamite and used as torpedoes to destroy enemy trains. Retreating armies tore up tracks to frustrate their pursuers. Tracklaying engineers and locomotive mechanics became as vital to the armies of the north as were horse soldiers.

In the northwest, Alvaro Obregón battled the federal

troops. Obregón, a science buff and an inventor, waged war in a starkly different manner from the hard-driving Pancho Villa. Before taking a town or a fortified hacienda, Obregón observed the terrain, captured the high ground overlooking his objective, and determined the best approach for his attacking soldiers. An avid reader, Obregón was familiar with the techniques of history's greatest commanders—Alexander the Great, Julius Caesar, and Napoléon. On the plains of northern Mexico, he deployed his troops with the skill of a master chess player.

As war spread over the land, successful armies grew in numbers, weapons, and strength. Guerrilla units from the hinterlands attached themselves to the best of the rebel divisions. Consequently, Obregón's became one of the most powerful armies in Mexico. The core of his soldiers remained the Yaqui Indians. They were grim-faced men, filled with hatred for Huerta, the federal troops, and for rich people in general. The Yaqui infantry fought as if death held little consequence. Guided by Obregón's brilliant tactics, the Yaquis and other troops were molded into an almost unbeatable army.

In theory, both Obregón and Villa were under the command of Venustiano Carranza, the self-proclaimed First Chief of the Revolution. Many of the orders issued by the First Chief, however, were ignored by the other two northern generals. Carranza had little appetite for war and hated field conditions. He traveled in a private three-car train with his private chef serving regular meals. In his

Venustiano Carranza

early 50s, he was considered to be an old man by his fellow revolutionaries, and he had a frustrating inability to make up his mind during a crisis. When asked for his views on a crucial matter, Carranza would comb his long white beard and then simply shrug his shoulders. Pancho Villa delighted in calling the First Chief "Old Goat

Whiskers." More of a politician than a warrior, Carranza longed to arrive in Mexico City, where the seat of governmental power lay.

To the south the Zapatistas were more an insurgent people than they were an army. Rarely did they fight battles on well-defined fronts. Instead the Zapatistas staged surprise raids against haciendas and small towns. When overwhelmed by federal troops, they cast aside their rifles and melted into the surroundings by becoming simple-minded, vague-talking country people. "Who is this fellow Zapata? Oh, maybe I heard the name, maybe not, but maybe yes, maybe." As long as they held on to their land, the Zapatistas were unconcerned about who was in power in Mexico City. They were driven only by a burning desire to retake the ejidos seized by hacienda owners. Zapata inspired his men with simple, direct statements: "Men of the south, it is better to die on your feet than to live on your knees."

The federal army suffered defeat after defeat against the rebel forces. The federal soldiers, most of whom were snatched off the streets of Mexico City and forced to serve, deserted in droves. As the army dissolved, the government in the Mexico City area ceased to function. Taxes went uncollected. Services came to a halt. Law gave way to anarchy.

Huerta was rarely seen in the presidential office. Instead he sat in one of his favorite downtown saloons, brooding over glasses of cognac. Living in Mexico City at the time was Edith O'Shaughnessy, the wife of an American diplomat. She wrote, "The task of peace seems well nigh hopeless. Huerta has very little natural regard for human life. This isn't a specialty of dictators anyway."

By early 1914 three-quarters of Mexico was in rebel hands. Huerta controlled only central Mexico and the Mexico City region. Turmoil reigned in the lands occupied by revolutionary forces. The revolutionaries opened jails and invited prisoners to join their ranks. Some prisoners served as soldiers, but hardened criminals used their newfound freedom to terrorize the countryside. As war raged over the land, mines went unattended, cattle were left to roam, and weeds overwhelmed corn patches. Family life splintered as men between 14 and 70 went off to fight. And the role of women in Mexican society underwent a profound change.

Prerevolutionary Mexican women were mothers and homemakers—little else. Even upper-class women went to school only long enough to learn basic reading and writing. Few professions were open to women. Laws forbade them from voting and restricted their right to own property. Mexico was a man's world where women were regarded as servants.

The demands of the Revolution, however, allowed Mexican women to gain new respect from men. The changes came gradually and were inspired by the lowly camp followers who traditionally traveled with Mexican armies. For generations women camp followers had

One of the many women who took part in the Mexican Revolution

attached themselves to Mexican soldiers. They foraged for food, cooked, and slept with the men. Often they had a baby strapped to their backs, but rarely were they married to the man they served. At the beginning of the Revolution, camp followers attached to the Constitutionalist army traded for food and other goods with camp followers who had assigned themselves to the federal units.

In the heat of combat, the camp followers found a new role. When their man fell from a bullet or shell splinter, the woman simply picked up his rifle and took his place on the battle line. If they survived the battle, many of the camp followers never returned to their old positions of servitude. Instead they became *soldaderas,* women soldiers. Shorthanded revolutionary commanders hardly cared if a woman served in the ranks alongside the men. Gradually the soldaderas assumed posts of leadership in the rebel armies. Every unit had a woman captain or major who led men into combat.

The Mexican philosopher Octavio Paz once called the uprising against Huerta a "fiesta of bullets." And at times the war took on a strange, festive atmosphere. Mexicans are among the most musical people on earth, and even the horrors of war could not diminish their desire to sing and dance. When the fighting was at a lull, soldiers' camps were full of song. A traveler could distinguish the various armies by the songs they favored. The Villistas preferred "Adelita," a spirited ballad about a girl with eyes "as green as the sea." The soldiers of Carranza sang "La Cucaracha," the story of a cockroach that did not know where it was going. One verse of the cucaracha song poked fun at the slightly overweight rival general Pancho Villa:

> *Una cosa me da risa,*
>> (One thing makes me laugh,)
> *Pancho Villa sin camisa.*
>> (Pancho Villa without his shirt.)

Still, Mexico was a hotbed of blood debts, and the fighting took on a nightmare quality. Years of the rich oppressing the poor and the whites lording over the non-whites planted seeds of hatred that blossomed into terrible wartime atrocities. The shooting of prisoners became a routine practice for all sides. At one point the Villistas were short of bullets, so they ordered their prisoners to stand in tight lines of three, one behind the other. That way one bullet fired through the chest of the first man killed all three. Months later Villa had plenty of ammunition, so he told one of his lieutenants, a vile little man named Rodolfo Fierro, to murder 300 captives with his pistol. Fierro gleefully did as he was ordered and later complained that his trigger finger developed a blister. In the south the Zapatistas dealt savagely with hacienda owners who put up a valiant fight. Some owners were nailed to the door of their manor house and left there to die. Other owners and hacienda foremen were staked over anthills to be eaten alive by the swarming insects.

Moving relentlessly southward, Pancho Villa's army was the Revolution's iron fist. Blocking Villa's advance was the city of Torreón, a vital railroad center defended by Huerta's best troops. "We will take Torreón with our teeth if need be," Villa declared. And after a furious struggle, Torreón fell. Nearer to Mexico City stood the ancient silver-mining town of Zacatecas, one of the last bastions of Huerta's strength. With pistol in hand, Villa led his

Dorados up sheer mountain cliffs and into the face of deadly rifle fire. Through raw courage and incredible force of will, Villa shot his way into the streets of Zacatecas. The federal soldiers, overwhelmed by this fanatical warrior, ran in panic.

Because of his daring, Villa, the bandit-turned-rebel, became a folk hero in the United States. American newspaper reporters followed his campaign and gave eyewitness accounts of the battles. Villa was portrayed as a dashing peasant leader on a noble crusade to uplift the masses and punish the Mexican rich who had for so long treated the workers like slaves. One of the most popular of these American journalists was John Reed, who rode with Villa for four months. "And where the fighting is fiercest," Reed wrote, "when a ragged mob of fierce brown men with hand bombs and rifles rush the bullet-swept streets of an ambushed town— Pancho Villa is among them like any common soldier."

After taking Zacatecas, Villa's army had swelled to 22,000 soldiers and soldaderas. This huge force was now posed to strike Mexico City.

But Venustiano Carranza, the First Chief, considered Mexico City to be his plum. Under no circumstances would he allow Villa to steal his thunder and enter the capital first. Carranza's army controlled the railroads linking Zacatecas with vital coal deposits. So Carranza stopped Villa's advance on Mexico City by ordering a halt to his coal deliveries. Without coal, Villa's trains could not run. Villa fumed and swore revenge on Carranza for this treacherous act. The generals of the north had been jealous of one another from the start of the war, but Carranza's coal embargo was their first major split.

In Mexico City, President Huerta packed his belongings and no doubt counted his money, too. During his 16-month tenure in office, millions of pesos in the national treasury had mysteriously disappeared. Facing a hopeless military situation, Huerta resigned as president in July 1914. Quietly he slipped out of Mexico and took a ship to Cuba. Later he traveled to the United States. He died in Texas in 1916 of cirrhosis of the liver, a disease brought about by alcoholism.

With Huerta gone, the people of Mexico City now waited, fearful of their fate. Who would occupy the capital? Would it be Pancho Villa, whose Dorados were known to rape women and carry off rich men for ransom? Or would the occupiers be Obregón and his hate-filled Yaqui Indians? While the Mexico City dwellers worried, the people of the countryside believed this was a time to rejoice. Huerta, the hideous dictator, was overthrown. The Constitutionalists had triumphed. At last the war, with all its violence, had come to an end. But victory celebrations in the country proved to be premature. The war now had an energy of its own, like a creature in a horror story, and that sinister energy grew with every drop of Mexican blood spilled on Mexican soil.

Chapter 7

GENERAL VERSUS GENERAL

......

What I can't get into my head is why we keep on fighting. Didn't we finish off this man Huerta?

—*A character in Mariano Azuela's novel of the Revolution,* The Underdogs

I n mid-August 1914, Alvaro Obregón and his fierce-looking Yaqui soldiers marched into Mexico City. The capital's middle class stayed at home behind locked doors, terrified because they believed Obregón's men were wanton murderers. Their fears proved to be baseless. Obregón declared the city to be under martial law and announced he would shoot all looters. The general from the north brought order to a city that had been in the grip of lawlessness since the last days of Huerta.

Obregón, however, had no love for Mexico City residents. He considered the men of Mexico City to be weaklings who cowered under the dictatorship of Huerta and let their country cousins do all the fighting. "It was inexcusable for you men to have abstained from taking up

The armies of Villa and Zapata enter Mexico City in triumph.

arms," Obregón told a Mexico City crowd that had gathered to pay homage to the slain president, Francisco Madero. Obregón then made a dramatic gesture that would live forever in the lore of the Revolution. Before an audience composed mainly of men, he gave his pistol to a young lady, a schoolteacher named María Arias, who had been a guerrilla fighter against the Huerta regime. "Since I know how to admire valor," Obregón said, "I cede my gun to this lady, the only person among you worthy to possess it." Forever afterward, María Arias was known as María Pistola, (Maria Pistol) and became a genuine heroine of the Revolution.

Venustiano Carranza arrived in Mexico City shortly after Obregón. The First Chief now claimed political leadership of the nation, which had been his goal since joining the conflict. In order to legitimatize his rule, Carranza ordered a convention to meet in the city of Aguascalientes. The convention was to decide the future of Mexican government. All the revolutionary leaders were invited. Carranza was confident he could dictate the terms of the convention. But a shocking development jarred his plans. Delegates loyal to Villa and Zapata took charge of the convention. They demanded radical land redistribution along the lines of Zapata's Plan of Ayala. Carranza, who was lukewarm about land reform, ordered his delegates to leave the convention. Sensing the coming of a war between the generals, Carranza and Obregón hastily left Mexico City to take refuge in Veracruz. Once more the capital was an open, unguarded city.

From the south came the Zapatistas, and from the north the Villistas swooped down upon Mexico City. Once more city residents waited, trembling in fear. Most of their dread was directed at the Zapatistas. The city-bred people considered Zapata's soldiers to be ignorant country brutes. Worse yet, the Zapata movement was so darkly *indio*—an Indian army led by a mostly Indian general. Since the time of the Spanish Conquest, the Mexico City elite had lived in fear of Indian uprisings. Now an upheaval was at their doorstep. The brown-skinned, dirt-scratching barbarians were converging on their unprotected city. Doom certainly was at hand.

They came not in military formation, but walking in small groups. The Zapatistas wore white cotton clothes, the uniform of the humble field hand. It was impossible to distinguish officers from men, or even soldiers from soldaderas. Many of the Zapatistas carried banners of the Virgin of Guadalupe, and they made the sign of the cross whenever they passed a church. All seemed awed by the towering buildings, the goods displayed in store windows, and the handsome statues that stood on the Paseo de la Reforma. When the markets closed, the Zapatistas knocked on doors and asked for—not demanded—food.

In early December 1914 the Villistas entered Mexico City, riding on boxcars that were peppered with bullet holes. At first the Villistas behaved well enough, but several of the men looted liquor stores, got drunk, and fired their rifles wildly in the air. Mexico City dwellers prayed future celebrations would not get more out of hand.

Zapata and Villa met for the first time in a Mexico City suburb. Although they shared similar goals, the two famous generals seemed uncomfortable in each other's

Generals Villa and Zapata meet in Mexico City. Villa is sitting in the president's chair.

presence. When they toured the National Palace, Villa sat in the president's chair, the Mexican republic's equivalent to a throne. Zapata was heard to mutter that the chair ought to be taken to the street and burned. Zapata left the capital shortly after his meeting with Villa. Most of the

Zapatistas followed the general back to Morelos, leaving Mexico City in the hands of the Villistas.

After their initial period of civilized behavior, the Villistas became a pack of fiends. They broke into stores and stole liquor and goods. Because of their leader's contempt for Catholic authority, churches were a special target for their escapades. Religious statues bedecked with gold and silver were snatched from altars. The horrible crime of rape was committed in all parts of the city, even on the open streets. Men who tried to rescue women being raped were shot. No woman was safe from attack.

The most notorious rape that took place during the occupation was committed by Pancho Villa himself. At the luxurious Hotel Palicio, Villa took a fancy to a young receptionist and announced he would return for her later. The terrified receptionist was sent home by the hotel manager, a refined Frenchwoman. When Villa came back, he could not find the receptionist. He turned to the Frenchwoman and said, "Then you'll have to do." The woman was beaten by Villa's bodyguards, then repeatedly raped by the revolutionary leader. The brutal crime became a worldwide scandal and forever stained the reputation of the onetime hero of the masses—Pancho Villa.

Villa and his troops soon drifted out of Mexico City, and Carranza and Obregón reoccupied the capital. The Mexican Revolution entered a crippling, demoralizing stage that saw generals fight one another for no purpose other than personal gain. In the months and years to come, Villa fought Obregón, Carranza fought Zapata, and finally Obregón fought Carranza. Dozens of lesser generals engaged in similar fratricidal wars. Mexico's agony continued without respite.

Combat during the wars between the generals was as ferocious as it had been in the past, but the spirit of revolution evaded the common soldier. Gone was the idealism that sent armies marching to the field to avenge Madero and topple the dictator Huerta. Men still uttered the battle cry "Land and Liberty," but the words now seemed empty. Soldiers fought for generals, not for causes. The war sped on, driven by its own momentum like a boulder bouncing downhill. Mexicans continued to kill one another, but no soldier could adequately explain the reason for the carnage. A character from *The Underdogs,* a novel written by a veteran of the Revolution, says, "You will ask me why I stay on in the revolution? The revolution is a hurricane. The man who is swept up in it is no longer a man; he is a wretched dry leaf snatched away by a gale."

The nation splintered into territories controlled by various generals. Within the territories the generals were the only law. They issued their own currencies and insisted their money was the only legal tender that could be used in the area they controlled. Villa's army traveled with a printing press on its troop train and printed thousands of bills with their commander's picture boldly on the face. At least 25 different forms of paper money—all worthless

outside the country—circulated in Mexico. Only the Zapatistas issued money of value. Zapata's men melted down
silver and made coins crudely stamped out on a hand-
press.

In the countryside the military strongmen became a
new ruling class. True, the generals uttered revolutionary
statements, but they made life as miserable for the
campesinos as did the property owners of previous years.
Wherever the armies traveled, they stripped the land bare
of produce and livestock. Many farmers simply gave up
their crops. They hoarded enough corn to feed their families but let their fields go to weeds. Men and women were
forced to join the marauding armies in order to get some-
thing to eat.

The year 1915, when the war between the generals
began, was known as the Year of Hunger in Mexico City.
With farm production down and various generals in control of the railroads, few food shipments reached the capital. Respectable people were forced to forage in garbage
cans, searching for morsels to eat. Boys and girls who had
once been well dressed became beggars and petty thieves.
Women of all ages turned to prostitution to obtain the
price of a few tortillas. Bodies of people who died in the
streets from starvation were picked up by death wagons
and taken to mass graves outside the city. The death wagons were among the few government services that still
functioned.

Through the veil of suffering that hung over the

nation, four leaders stood out—Villa, Zapata, Carranza, and Obregón. Of the four, only Zapata had no desire to become president of Mexico. Villa was a field commander, and the art of political leadership escaped him. Obregón had his eye on the president's chair, but he was willing to wait for his opportunity. This left Carranza at the top of a very shaky ladder.

The most serious threat facing Carranza was Pancho Villa, who commanded a large and well-equipped army. Against Villa, Carranza could counter with Obregón and his highly disciplined Yaqui troops. Carranza and Obregón remained allies, though neither man liked or trusted the other. Obregón agreed to go to the field and destroy the army of Pancho Villa. The stage was set for the bloodiest battle of the Mexican Revolution.

It would seem that Villa had all the advantages in the coming fight. His army outnumbered Obregón's by at least three to one. However, Obregón was a brilliant strategist. He knew that Villa was in a foul mood and could be coaxed into battle on unfavorable terms. Also, Obregón had studied reports written by commanders fighting the awful trench warfare taking place at the time in Europe. The reports spelled out in deadly clarity that modern machine guns firing 600 bullets a minute were instruments that killed on a ghastly scale.

Near the lovely colonial town of Celaya, Obregón ordered his men to dig trenches. In front of the trenches he ran coils of barbed wire. At regular intervals he placed batteries of his newest machine guns. Obregón transformed the Mexican corn patches into an eerie likeness of a World War I battlefield. Celaya is a little more than 100 miles north of Mexico City. A better tactician than Villa would have lured his opponent farther north to stretch out his supply lines. Villa, however, was as eager to attack as Obregón hoped he would be.

With bugles blaring and cries of "Viva Pancho Villa!" the battle of Celaya began on April 6, 1915. Following his foremost military instinct—charge!—Villa led some 30,000 cavalry and foot soldiers racing toward Obregón's entrenched infantry. The result was butchery. Obregón's machine guns blazed in carefully prepared crisscross lines of fire. The attackers who survived the deadly rain of machine gun bullets became entangled in barbed wire. Horses and men screamed in terror and agony. Inside the trenches lay Obregón's fearless Yaqui riflemen. Yaqui wives, girlfriends, and children also occupied the trenches, where they busily reloaded rifles. When a Yaqui man fell victim to a Villista bullet, the woman picked up the rifle. When she fell, the rifle was passed to the oldest boy.

The battle of Celaya lasted three days. Villa fought in the same manner that made him the feared Dorado of the north. Again and again he charged Obregón's trenches. But his fury was no match against the cool mind of Obregón and the determination of the Yaqui defenders. Four thousand Villistas were killed at Celaya and 6,000 were taken prisoner.

General Alvaro Obregón after his shattered arm was amputated.

The Villistas retreated and the two revolutionary divisions clashed again, this time at the nearby city of León. The battle of León was another Obregón victory, but the commander became a casualty when an exploding shell tore off his right arm. Obregón was in such maddening pain that he drew his pistol, pointed it at his heart, and pulled the trigger. "I hoped to finish the work the shell had begun," Obregón later wrote. The gun did not fire, however, and quick medical attention saved his life.

Villa withdrew to northern Mexico. There, in his familiar mountains, his army was invincible. But never again would Pancho Villa ride at the head of the feared Dorados and terrorize his enemies.

In Mexico City, Carranza was delighted with Villa's defeat. Carranza now shifted his attention to the south. He still had to deal with Zapata and his stubborn peasant army.

During 1915, while the generals of the north battled one another, the Zapatistas organized a separate society in the south. In effect, they declared Morelos and their southern territory to be independent from the rest of Mexico. Under the guidelines of the Plan of Ayala, the great haciendas of the south were broken up and local people were given land. In addition to their land program, the Zapatistas ran sugar mills and operated an arms factory that refurbished old rifles.

With the intent of crushing Zapata's country within a country, Carranza sent General Pablo González to the south. González was an ambitious man who also thirsted to be president. So far, however, he had failed miserably in combat. González was known as "the general who never won a battle," and the nickname was all too appropriate. But what González lacked in generalship he overcame in meanness and treachery.

Upon arriving in Morelos, General González launched a scorched earth campaign designed to starve out the Zapatistas. He burned crops, shot cattle, and blew up bridges used by farmers. Employing terror tactics, he hanged hundreds of campesinos suspected to be Zapata sympathizers. Yet he had no more success at stopping the campesino rebellion than did generals under Díaz or Huerta. Although González managed to retake the cities, the countryside belonged to the white-clad peasants who worshiped Zapata as if he were a saint. Surrounded by these closemouthed, utterly dedicated people, Emiliano Zapata was untouchable.

The war between the generals loomed as a powder keg for American president Woodrow Wilson. American corporations owned more than $1 billion worth of property and machinery in Mexico. Continued warfare meant that American oil wells were not pumping and that American cattle ranches were being raided by warring generals. Businessmen urged the president to send the United States army to Mexico to stop the war and protect American interests.

Wilson tried to end the war between the generals by

throwing his support behind the one man who seemed to be in the strongest position to win—Venustiano Carranza. In October 1915, Wilson announced the United States would recognize Carranza as the legitimate president of Mexico. He forbade American arms merchants from selling weapons to any of Carranza's rival generals. Wilson's support of Carranza infuriated Pancho Villa. Villa believed the American president had stabbed him in the back, and he swore revenge.

Under the cover of darkness, Pancho Villa led 485 horsemen across the American border. It was March 1916. Villa and his men headed toward the town of Columbus, New Mexico. He was determined to raid an American city for two reasons: First, he wanted to punish the Americans; second, he hoped to embarrass the Carranza government. At dawn, Villa and his followers stormed down Columbus's main street, whooping, yelling, and firing wildly. Sixteen Americans were killed during the assault. The American public was outraged. Villa—a onetime hero in the eyes of many Americans—had killed United States citizens on American soil. The people cried out for vengeance.

President Wilson sent a force of 6,000 army troops into Mexico to capture Villa "alive or dead." The unit was led by General John Pershing, the nation's foremost cavalry commander. In Mexico City an angry president Carranza denounced the border crossing as "an invasion," but there was little he could do against the U.S. Army.

Villa in the mountains of Mexico while in hiding from American troops

Pershing had no success at all in finding the elusive Villa. Even with the assistance of airplanes, which had never been seen before in the skies over northern Mexico, Villa still escaped his pursuers. He even joked at the American effort to find him in his mountain lairs. When Villa was told the Americans, as a reward, had put up a 50,000-peso price on his head, he said, "So many pesos for so little a head."

All over the country Mexicans delighted in the Americans' inability to capture Villa, who was an enigmatic figure in Mexican history. He was a brute who considered rape to be a legitimate method of seducing a woman. He was a cold-blooded killer who was known to laugh while gunning down another man. But he also sat in the dirt eating his meals with common soldiers. And he was able to outfox an American general and make fools of an entire Yankee army. For those reasons, he is a hero of sorts in the lore of Mexico.

General Pershing withdrew from Mexico in January 1917 after chasing Villa for ten frustrating months. President Wilson recalled the army because he believed Pershing and his men would soon be sent overseas to fight against Germany. One of the reasons for worsening relations with Germany was a telegram sent by the German foreign secretary, Arthur Zimmermann, to the Carranza government. The Zimmermann Telegram urged Mexico to attack the United States and "reconquer her lost territory in Texas, New Mexico, and Arizona." The note did not have the backing of the German government. In fact, it was little more than a harebrained scheme dreamed up by Secretary Zimmermann. Still, the Zimmermann Telegram caused sensational headlines when it was intercepted by the British and handed over to American authorities. Five weeks later, America declared war on Germany.

As 1916 came to a close, the war between the generals still smoldered, but Mexico was exhausted after years of bloodshed. The generals sensed that an uneasy peace was beginning to take hold of the land. Now they scrambled to consolidate their powers.

Chapter 8

The
TWILIGHT
of the
GENERALS
.....

**[He was] a great man for little things
and a small man for great ones.**

—*Alvaro Obregón, speaking of
President Venustiano Carranza*

y early 1917 the fighting fury on the fields of Mexico slowed down like a car running out of gas. Mexicans were simply too fatigued to carry on warfare with the mad intensity of the past.

Politically an uneasy peace settled over Mexico City. Carranza emerged, at least temporarily, as the winner in the war between the generals. Villa had been reduced to a life of banditry in northern Mexico. Zapata's peasant rebellion remained in force, but the Zapatistas were unlikely to march to the capital and overthrow the president. Obregón was Carranza's only serious rival, and he was cagily waiting his turn to seize national leadership.

Some 500 lesser generals still commanded armies. Carranza began pacifying the minor generals in a time-honored fashion—by paying them off. One general might be given a huge ranch, while another was awarded a lucrative job in national or state government. The reforms promised by the Revolution—land and justice—were ignored by Carranza as he distributed the spoils of the nation to military strongmen. But Carranza was determined to deliver on one promise.

Carranza and the other generals of the north had fought as Constitutionalists. They claimed their primary goal in waging revolutionary war was to give the nation a constitution to serve as the framework for a more enlightened government. Carranza called for a constitutional convention to meet at the city of Querétaro. Villa and Zapata supporters were not invited. This time Carranza was confident he could dictate the terms of the convention. He favored a rewritten version of the 1857 constitution, which called for the separation of church and state and no reelection of presidents. Carranza instructed his delegates to steer clear of the land redistribution issue. He and most of his friends were property owners who had no desire to see their haciendas and ranches swallowed up by landless peasants. But as was true with the previous convention in Aguascalientes, the Querétaro meeting soon slipped out of Carranza's control.

The constitution writers who met in Querétaro in December 1916 were middle-class men: teachers, lawyers, and shopkeepers. They were not radicals who demanded the immediate confiscation of property belonging to the rich. Yet they had a conscience. They believed they could not offer the nation a rewritten version of a 60-year-old constitution after the people had suffered through such terrible bloodletting. So the delegates scrapped the 1857 constitution and wrote a new charter. It turned out to be an amazing document whose principles govern the nation to this day.

The new constitution was written in six weeks and approved on February 5, 1917. In many respects it was progressive beyond a reformer's dreams. Most Mexican progressives wanted strict separation between church and state. On that issue its language was rigid. The constitution decreed all education was to be public, all marriages civil, and that churches were not allowed to own land other than the ground the church stood upon. The constitution's Article 123 recognized the right of Mexican workers to form labor unions. Article 123 also limited the workday to eight hours, prohibited child labor, and established a minimum wage. No other nation in 1917 had such far-reaching workers' rights written directly into the constitution.

The hottest question facing the delegates at Querétaro was that of land redistribution—the basic cause of the Revolution. Article 27 of the Constitution of 1917 gave the government the right to redistribute land as government authorities saw fit. However, this article also meant that a government like Carranza's, that favored the hacienda owners, could drag its feet on land reform. Another clause in Article 27 stated that the wealth of the subsoil—minerals and oil—may be used only by Mexicans or by foreigners willing to obey all Mexican laws. This clause put severe restrictions on foreign companies that owned oil wells and silver mines in Mexico.

Venustiano Carranza viewed the Constitution of 1917 as a radical document. It became his policy to simply ignore much of what the constitution promised. For example, the constitution required the government to provide an education through the primary grades for all Mexican children. But Carranza's education budget was only slightly higher than Díaz's. Carranza also looked the other way at the clause that forbade child labor. As a result, Mexican children continued to go to work at the age of nine or ten, never seeing the inside of a classroom.

Running virtually unopposed, Carranza was elected president in March 1917. In the south the Zapatistas refused to recognize him as their leader. Addressing the president as "citizen Carranza," Zapata wrote, "From the time you first...named yourself Chief [of the Revolution], you proceeded to turn the struggle to the advantage of yourself and the friends and allies who helped you climb and then shared the booty—riches, honors, businesses, banquets, sumptuous fiestas....It never entered your mind that the Revolution was for the benefit of the great masses....You took justice in your own hands and created a dictatorship which you gave the name 'Revolution.'"

The letter infuriated Carranza, and he ordered General Pablo González to crush the Zapatista movement once and for all. González stepped up his scorched earth campaign and his war of terror against the campesinos. Reasoning that the Zapatistas lived off the peasants, González attempted to remove the peasants from the land. Through mass murder and forced deportation, he reduced the population of Morelos by 40 percent. Still, the campesinos who remained were willing to fight for Zapata until death. Small bands of farmers raided González's supply dumps, attacked his trains, and ambushed his troops.

Failing in his attempts to best Zapata in battle, González resorted to a desperate trick. He ordered one of his officers, a colonel named Jesús Guajardo, to approach Zapata secretly, posing as a turncoat. Through friendly farmers, Guajardo passed the word that he was anxious to switch sides and join the rebels with all his men and their weapons. Such defections were common in revolutionary Mexico. To demonstrate his sincerity, the colonel arranged to fight a sham battle against a detachment of González's men. Guajardo easily won the "battle" and then had 59 prisoners shot. Zapata decided to take a chance on the colonel's promise to defect, because he desperately needed replacement soldiers and modern weapons.

An arrangement was made for Zapata to meet Colonel Guajardo at an abandoned hacienda. As Zapata and ten men approached the hacienda walls, the soldiers inside saluted him with a bugle call. One of the ten men riding with Zapata described the scene: "Three times the bugle sounded the honor call, and as the last note died away, as

[our leader] reached the door…the soldiers who were pre-
senting arms fired two volleys, and our unforgettable
General Zapata fell, never to rise again."

Emiliano Zapata was killed on the morning of April
10, 1919. His body, torn by scores of bullets, was carried
on the back of a mule to the central square at the city of
Cuautla. There it was tied to a post, where it remained for
several days. Word passed from one tiny village to another that the beloved man the people called 'Miliano had
been shot and that his body was on display. Thousands of
campesinos flocked from the countryside to see for themselves if this awful news was true. At Cuautla's square they
saw him, lifeless, stiff, the blood caking on his white shirt.
Still they refused to believe what they saw. Their 'Miliano
could not die. He would march with the peasants
always—forever.

President Carranza was delighted when he heard that
Zapata had been killed. He promoted the deceitful
Colonel Guajardo to the rank of general and gave him a
bonus of 50,000 pesos.

In early 1920 Carranza's term of office was due to
expire. Since one of his strongest principles was "no
reelection," he could not reasonably ask the public to give
him another term. But Carranza was not a man to simply
step down from a position of power. Before new elections
were scheduled, he threw his support to a political
unknown named Ignacio Bonillas, Mexico's ambassador
to Washington. Bonillas had spent so much time in the

United States away from his own country that Mexicans joked his name was not Señor Bonillas, but Meester Bonillas. It was clear to all what Carranza was trying to accomplish. He wanted Bonillas to become president and act as his puppet while he remained the real power behind the government.

Carranza, however, underestimated the influence and popularity enjoyed by his longtime rival Alvaro Obregón. In 1920 Obregón felt he deserved the office of the president. Most of the Mexican public agreed. Because of Carranza's shady attempt to remain in power, Mexico was shaken by revolutionary armed force once again. In the state of Sonora, generals allied with Obregón declared rebellion and started marching their armies south. The marchers grew in number as more and more generals joined the anti-Carranza crusade.

Fearing for his life, Carranza made plans to abandon Mexico City and travel to Veracruz, where he hoped to form a new government. With a staff that included cooks, servants, and a few loyal officers, Carranza boarded a 21-car train to make the journey. With him were sacks containing five million pesos in gold and silver. Carranza had taken the money from the national treasury hoping to use it to pay soldiers and raise a new army.

The trip to Veracruz proved to be a calamity. The Carranza party became stranded in the state of Puebla because troops loyal to Obregón had blown up the train tracks. Forced to abandon the train, Carranza and his staff continued the journey on horseback. At every remote mountain village, Carranza attracted a huge crowd, not because he was president but because in desperation he began giving away fistfuls of gold to any man willing to join his army. One officer in the party recalled in amazement, "[The people] filled their pockets with gold, only to discover it was the worst possible thing they could have done because their horses were too loaded down to ride. And so they tried to rid themselves of the gold by giving it to everyone in their path....It really is true what they tell you as a child...that money is worth nothing. It is truly worthless compared to saving your life."

As he fled over the rugged mountains of Puebla, Carranza paid a local chieftain named Rodolfo Herrera to protect him from his many enemies. Herrera assured the president he was safe in his region. He guided Carranza and his few remaining men to a remote mountain shack where he told the president he could get a good night's sleep. An exhausted Venustiano Carranza agreed to sleep in the shack, even though he preferred more comfortable quarters. During the night, Herrera, who was secretly an Obregón loyalist, shot and killed Carranza. Herrera later announced the president had committed suicide.

Once more a powerful army descended on Mexico City and marched down the Paseo de la Reforma. But this time Mexico City dwellers did not cringe in fear. These were troops from Sonora, all of them loyal to Alvaro Obregón. Many Mexicans wept for joy when they saw the men. Even those who disliked Obregón recognized him as a no-nonsense political leader who would finally bring order to a nation torn asunder. Alvaro Obregón was not what the revolutionaries had demanded many bloody years ago, but he was the only leader with the political skills needed to usher in a new Mexico.

Chapter 9

A
NEW
SOCIETY

. . . . .

Pancho Villa had surrendered
In the city of Torreón,
He is tired now of fighting
And now the cotton will be grown.

Now we are all one country
There is no one left to fight;
The war had ended, *compañeros,*
Let us work, it is our right.

—A village song popular in the 1920s

Alvaro Obregón was elected president in September of 1920. His ascendency to the office marked the end of the warfare that had gripped the nation for ten years. Obregón was not a firebrand revolutionary. Instead he was a practical politician, determined to bring peace to a battered land.

As president, Obregón continued Carranza's policy of demilitarization by rewarding generals if they agreed to disarm. This practice led to widespread corruption as many of the military strongmen were given government

ASESINATO
DEL GENERAL
FRANCISCO VILLA

Villa's life ended in a rain of bullets when assassins ambushed his car.

jobs. Once comfortably in office, the generals-turned-politicians raided the treasury as readily as they used to plunder rich haciendas.

In the north, Pancho Villa was bribed into dissolving his army with the gift of a 26,000-acre ranch. Enjoying life as a prosperous rancher, Villa became as greedy as the hacienda owners of the Díaz era. He hired thugs to gun down a group of peasants who tried to move onto the fringe areas of his land. Some of the campesinos who were killed were onetime members of Villa's own army. Villa was killed in 1923, when his car was ambushed and raked with gunfire. Some people claimed government agents were behind the murder, while others maintained Villa was shot by angry campesinos who coveted his ranch.

On land reform, Obregón moved slowly. He established a legal process by which villagers could reclaim land taken from them by the haciendas, but the appeals of the peasants were often tied up for years in a cumbersome court system. Only in the state of Morelos, where the memory of Emiliano Zapata burned in the minds of militant farmers, did land reform proceed smoothly.

Knowing he would never be popular with small farmers, President Obregón established strong ties with the nation's labor movement. The most powerful labor organization was the *Confederación Regional Obrera Mejicana,* better known as the CROM. The CROM was a collection of trade unions that grew from a membership of 50,000 to 1.2 million during Obregón's four years in office. The organization helped secure better wages for its members, but it was rotten with corruption. By collecting union dues and bribes from companies, CROM's leader, Luis Morones, acquired mansions and a fleet of automobiles. Morones, however, could be relied upon to do favors for Obregón. When the president needed a rally to support a policy, the CROM was always willing to serve as his political arm.

Obregón dismissed pocket stuffing among union leaders and politicians as the hard price of peace. Sometimes he joked about the corruption staining his administration. Once, referring to the arm he had lost during the war, Obregón said, "All of us [politicians] are thieves, more or less. However, I have only one hand [with which to steal], while the others have two. That is why the people prefer me."

Though the massive clash of armies had ended, tempers still stewed in Obregón's Mexico. Militant Catholics battled in the streets with anticlerical revolutionaries. A growing Socialist and Communist movement urged mob action to steer Mexico on a more radical course. Also, many generals threatened to renew the war because they were unsatisfied with their rewards for disarming. Obregón was harsh in dealing with upstart generals or radicals. Execution by firing squad was a common practice during his administration. The president had no love for summary executions, but he considered them necessary in the land still inflamed with revolutionary violence. "People are pacified with laws," he once said, "and laws are defended with rifles."

To his credit, Obregón launched a vigorous effort to educate all Mexican children. He also granted freedom of expression to artists and writers. The freedoms he unleashed stimulated a bold new society.

Obregón's supreme stroke of genius was the appointment of José Vasconcelos as his secretary of education. A complex, intellectual, and passionate man, Vasconcelos looked upon the education of Mexican youth as a holy crusade. Under his leadership money devoted to public education became the largest single item in the national budget for the first time in Mexico's history. Vasconcelos ordered more than 1,000 new schools to be built, many in rural areas so primitive they lacked even a road. When groups of young men and women graduated from teachers' colleges, Vasconcelos himself gave them fiery speeches and sent the young teachers marching into Mexico's hinterlands with the spirit of missionaries dispatched by the church.

Vasconcelos held a profound belief that learning to read must become the birthright of all Mexicans. He established government printing houses and shipped millions of textbooks to the school systems. As a scholar, Vasconcelos favored the classics. So, soon after a child mastered rudimentary reading, he or she was given a copy of the works of Plato or Aristotle to study.

Obregón, a purely practical man, thought that force-feeding the classics to children who came from generations of illiterates was an exercise in folly. But the president gave Vasconcelos a free hand in his efforts to uplift the people. He was even able to smile at his education secretary's zeal for the works of ancient Greece. Obregón once met an old man at a train station who was so unlettered he could not even name the village where he lived. The president joked to his aide, "Give this man five pesos and tell Vasconcelos to send him a copy of Plato."

Following Madero's precedent, Obregón freed the press from all censorship. In addition to newspapers, poetry magazines and theater groups were given liberty to lampoon and criticize the postrevolutionary government. The new spirit of freedom fostered a sparkling creative movement in Mexican literature. The war that had just concluded was the biggest and bloodiest event in the nation's history. Many of its participants—from the generals to the common soldiers—hungered to tell their part in this epic story. In the excitement of the new society, a flood of books poured forth.

Certainly the classic novel written about the Mexican Revolution was *Los de Abajo* (translated as *The Underdogs*), by Mariano Azuela. Azuela was a doctor who served with the army of Pancho Villa. His book tells the story of a simple peasant caught up in the whirlwind of revolutionary warfare. Initially the peasant has no clear idea why he is fighting. When the war degenerates into the general versus general stage, the man has simply become drunk on its mad violence: "Villa? Obregón? Carranza? What's the difference? I love the revolution like a volcano in eruption. I love the volcano because it's a volcano, the revolution because it's a revolution."

Azuela was disappointed with the results of the Mexican Revolution. Although the people had endured incredible suffering and loss of life, they were as poor now as they were before the war. Azuela concluded that Mexicans were betrayed by the Revolution's leaders because in the postwar years the leaders lived in luxury while the people struggled. To him the Mexican Revolution, like so many other wars in history, was one where the idealists were killed while the opportunists reaped rewards.

The Revolution also stimulated American journalism. American readers followed the movement of revolutionary armies with amazement, much as they would follow a sporting event. The Yankee journalists who braved bullets and shells to bring the story home were hailed as heroes. One of the most popular American writers in Mexico was John Reed, who attached himself to Villa's army. Reed was known to scribble out stories even when rifle fire rained down upon him. An ardent Communist, Reed later covered the Russian Revolution and became a hero in the Soviet state. More than one million Americans read John Kenneth Turner's book *Barbarous Mexico,* which described the horrible conditions in labor camps before the war. Turner's book became akin to *Uncle Tom's Cabin* and served in American minds as a justification for the great rebellion in Mexico.

The most mysterious of the Yankee writers in Mexico was Ambrose Bierce. As a young man, Bierce fought in the American Civil War. Ever since that awful experience, he was haunted by nightmare visions of corpses rotting on battlefields. Bierce's short stories were macabre tales that featured supernatural creatures and told of death in shocking terms. In 1914, Bierce, then an old man in his 70s, traveled to Mexico to write about the war. Somewhere in northern Mexico he disappeared. Neither his body nor his grave were ever discovered. Bierce simply faded away into legend.

Mexico's new society electrified the world with its contributions to art. For generations talented Mexican artists had labored to copy the techniques used by the European masters. Then the Revolution caused a new fire to burn in the Mexican soul. Postrevolutionary art embraced exciting, purely Mexican themes. Paintings appeared showing villages where people ate tortillas instead of bread. The Mexican love for bright colors and wild forms burst out of canvasses. And the greatest of the postrevolutionary artists turned their attention to murals—an ancient Mexican tradition.

Murals are wall paintings that adorn buildings. In pre-Columbian Mexico, Indian artists painted complex pictures on the walls of their temples and pyramids. After the Spanish Conquest the Indians, now joined with mestizo artists, painted stunning religious scenes inside Catholic churches. The Mexican muralist tradition flowered again in the 1920s. Education Secretary José Vasconcelos, who acted as a cultural czar over the nation, encouraged the mural movement by commissioning the best artists to paint the walls of public buildings. The three master muralists of the time were José Clemente Orozco, David

Alfaro Siqueiros, and Diego Rivera. These "Big Three" became idols in Mexico. Critics around the world hailed their work as among the finest ever conceived on the American continent.

David Siqueiros was the youngest of the Big Three. He served as an officer in the revolutionary army when he was still a teenager. A devoted Communist, he painted scenes of once backward villagers who elevated themselves through their work and took an honored place in the modern industrial world. "We have had enough of pretty pictures of grinning peasants in traditional dress and carrying baskets on their backs," he said. "I say to hell with the ox carts—let's see more tractors and bulldozers." A fighter and rebel all his life, Siqueiros spent several years in jail for Communist activities. In terms of pure talent, Siqueiros might have been the greatest of the Big Three, but his passion for politics was as powerful as his yearning to paint. Because he was constantly running off to attend political rallies, he left many of his works unfinished.

Older and not so interested in politics was José Clemente Orozco. He grew up in Mexico City, and his early paintings showed a fascination with the capital's seedy nightlife. "Instead of red and yellow twilights I painted drunken ladies and gentlemen," he once wrote. Many of Orozco's fellow painters tried to depict Mexico's revolutionary war as a golden chapter in the country's history. To Orozco, however, the war was wasteful carnage. He was one of the many artists and writers who believed

A self-portrait by David Alfaro Siqueiros, one of the many Mexican artists to draw inspiration from the events of the Mexican Revolution.

the Revolution's leaders had broken faith with the people. Orozco portrayed war as a horrific experience, never as a field of glory.

In the eyes of the Mexican public, Diego Rivera was the country's greatest artist of all. Common people worshiped Rivera much as modern Americans adore a baseball player or movie star. His antics in Mexico City night-clubs and his many love affairs were reported in detail in the national press. Rivera stood six feet tall and weighed a beefy 300 pounds. Sporting an unkempt beard and usual-ly wearing paint-stained clothes, he described himself as "attractively ugly." Despite his tattered appearance, the

An Aztec is branded by a Spanish conquistador, as depicted in a mural by Mexican artist Diego Rivera.

artist had an almost magnetic effect on women. The most beautiful women in Mexican society and debutantes from Europe and the United States waited outside his studio in the hope that the great man would at least smile or say hello to them. Rivera, a womanizer by nature, had new girlfriends whenever he desired them. These romantic escapades infuriated Rivera's wife, Frida Kahlo, who was herself a talented artist. Frida sometimes fought in public with Diego, but more often she smothered her sorrows by devoting herself to her work. Her paintings are now as famous as those of her husband.

Education Secretary José Vasconcelos instructed the muralists to concentrate on Mexican history as their primary theme for public buildings. Aside from the general direction of history, Vasconcelos gave the muralists the freedom to paint whatever they wished. Siqueiros preferred blatantly pro-Communist themes. Orozco glorified the historic meeting between Spaniards and Indians that created the mestizo race. Rivera, on the other hand, praised Indian civilization as a lost paradise and condemned the Spaniards as brutal slave masters.

Rivera's most famous historical mural adorns the wall of the National Palace at the Zocalo. On the left side of the mural, pre-Columbian Indians are seen peacefully building pyramids and raising crops. Two dogs in the pre-Columbian scene are romping playfully. The right side of the mural shows hideous-looking Spaniards putting the Indians in chains and branding one of them on the face with a red-hot iron. The two dogs that were once merrily at play now snarl at each other fang to fang.

The work of the muralists met with praise as well as with bitter denunciations. Mexico was still a nation at war with itself, even though no armies battled in the fields. When the muralists exalted communism or when they damned the Catholic church, they touched on raw nerves. Mexico City dwellers, offended by the muralists' themes, threw rocks at the artists while they labored over their paintings. Art students defending the master muralists got into fistfights with outraged citizens.

Yet the muralists—loved or hated for their works—remained national heroes for decades to come. When José Clemente Orozco died of a heart attack in 1949, an American visitor was astonished to see Mexico City factory workers, waitresses, and taxi drivers weeping on the streets. The American wrote, "What a wonderful thing it was for an artist to be a citizen of a country where, if he was a great artist, he could also be a great man."

Chapter 10

In the
WAKE
of
WAR
......

The Revolution was the sudden immersion of Mexico in her own being, from which she brought back up, almost blindly, the essentials of a new kind of state.

—The Mexican philosopher Octavio Paz

bregón's new society and the excitement generated by its literature and art could not cover up the wounds of war. Buildings in every city and village were reduced to rubble or at least pockmarked with bullet holes. Farms were in such a state of disruption that Mexico grew only one-tenth the amount of corn it needed to feed its people.

Worse yet was the war's tremendous cost in human lives. As many as two million Mexicans—one in every eight of the population—had died either in battle or from the disease and famine brought about by warfare. The ten-year span from 1910 to 1920 was the only decade in modern Mexican history that saw the population decrease rather than rise. In terms of loss of life, the Mexican Revolution was the costliest war ever fought on the American

A pile of charred bodies symbolizes the thousands of deaths that occurred during the bloody Revolution.

continent, dwarfing even the great Civil War that took place in the United States.

People around the world asked, Did Mexico reap any benefits from this appallingly bloody war? On the surface it appeared the people gained nothing. Most campesinos remained landless. The nation as a whole was poorer than it was under Porfirio Díaz. Foreign observers concluded the Revolution was a waste.

But it took a Mexican to notice the subtle changes

that had crept into the nation's society as a result of the Revolution. The war broke the bonds of the past and altered the nation's mind and spirit. Gone was the caste system that separated Mexicans into whites, mestizos, and Indians and left many people—especially the Indians—strangers in their own land. Mexicans had suffered a period of horror and now emerged together hand in hand, like the survivors of a hurricane or an earthquake. The calamity of war assured that there would never again be a return to the old days. Yes, the Indians and the mestizos for the most part remained poorer than the whites, but now all were Mexicans. After the war the nation was more unified than it had ever been before in its history.

Because the changes ushered in by the Revolution affected only Mexicans, the whole spectacular episode is a footnote rather than a headline in world history. The Russian Revolution of 1917 impacted the world because for a 70-year period Communist leaders tried to export their insurrection to other nations. The American Revolution of 1776 and the French Revolution, which began in 1789, fired the passions of liberty-loving people for centuries to come. The echoes of the Mexican Revolution—though they were profound—stayed at home, appreciated mostly by the people of Mexico.

The Mexican philosopher Octavio Paz claims the Revolution was a hammer blow that enabled Mexico to shatter the almost feudal society it maintained in the past and rise to become a modern state. In his book *The Labyrinth of Solitude,* Paz explains, "Our Revolution is the other face of Mexico....It is not the face of courtesy....It is the brutal, resplendent face of death and fiestas, of gossip and gunfire. And with whom does Mexico commune in this bloody fiesta? With herself, with her own being. Mexico dares to exist, to be. The revolutionary explosion is a prodigious fiesta in which the Mexican, drunk with his own self, is aware at last, in a mortal embrace, of his fellow Mexicans."

Postwar politics remained turbulent, but at least a semblance of order prevailed. Obregón's term of office expired in 1924, and Plutarco Elías Calles was elected president. When Calles took office, it marked the first peaceful change of presidents that Mexico had experienced in more than 40 years.

During the war, Calles had been an Obregón supporter. As president he continued Obregón's policies, especially the program to build schools in rural areas. But Calles lacked Obregón's charm and sense of humor. He interpreted criticism from the press or from political opponents as personal insults. And Calles harbored an almost insane hatred toward the Catholic church.

Throughout the revolutionary years most leaders claimed to be anticlerical. But their condemnation of the church often left a bitter taste in the mouths of their followers. Mexicans are a deeply religious people, and the vast majority are devoted Catholics. President Calles pushed the Mexican conscience too far when he deported

Plutarco Elías Calles

100 priests and nuns and closed all the nation's remaining religious schools. To protest these actions, the Catholic church went on strike in 1926. Church leaders ordered priests not to celebrate mass, perform marriages, or render any other church services. The strike lasted for three years, and during that time, not one church bell chimed

in Mexico. Anyone who has lived in the country can appreciate the emptiness the villagers must have felt at being deprived of their cherished bells.

Because of Calles's repression of the church, a short-lived uprising called the Cristero Rebellion broke out in 1927. Crying out "Viva Cristo Rey!" ("Long Live Christ the King!"), the Cristeros burned government schools and murdered officials. Calles, who was a dictator at heart, sent the army to crush the rebellion. Hundreds of Cristeros were hanged from telephone poles. Historians regard the Cristero movement as the last wave of violence to wash over Mexico from the high tide of the great upheaval.

Calles's term expired in 1928, and Alvaro Obregón, who was still a popular leader, won reelection to office. Three weeks after the election, Obregón ate dinner with friends at a suburban Mexico City restaurant. A young, well-dressed man with a sketch pad drew pictures of several guests in the Obregón party. The artist asked the president-elect if he could draw him, too. Obregón agreed. He had no idea the artist was a Catholic fanatic who hated Obregón because he had made many anticlerical speeches. The artist pulled a pistol from his jacket and fired five times into Obregón's face. The president-elect died instantly.

Just a few years earlier, an incident such as Obregón's assassination would have thrown the country into renewed revolution. But now the peace was unbroken. The government was dominated by a powerful political machine set up by former president Calles. With the machine's blessings a succession of three presidents held office, each serving a two-year term. They were mere puppets of Calles, and Mexicans called them "straw men." Then, in 1934, a state governor named Lázaro Cárdenas was elected president. He defied the Calles machine and became the greatest Mexican president of the 20th century.

Cárdenas was a teenager when the Mexican Revolution broke out. He organized a band of soldiers and joined Obregón's army. As president he displayed a commitment to the poor never before seen in a Mexican political leader. He routinely rode on burro-back to the nation's most remote areas to listen to the problems faced by the farmers. During his term in office, he redistributed more hacienda land to the villagers than had all the previous postrevolutionary presidents combined. In 1938, Cárdenas shocked the economic world by nationalizing Mexico's oil, thereby claiming all oil fields to be the property of the state. This action infuriated American companies, but Mexicans were overjoyed by the president's boldness. The adoration the Mexican people felt for Lázaro Cárdenas spanned the decades. His son, Cuauhtémoc Cárdenas, was a popular political leader in the 1980s and 1990s and was almost elected president.

By the end of Lázaro Cárdenas's term of office in 1940, memories of the great upheaval had faded. Children learned of the Revolution from stories told by their grandparents. Also, revolutionary deeds were celebrated in fiestas. During fiesta time, children, dressed as soldiers, refought battles in the village square while rockets burst overhead. Aging soldiers and soldaderas smiled at the mock combat.

The fiestas brought long-dead heroes back to life. A boy dressed as Pancho Villa would be chased around the square by another boy dressed as American general Pershing. Always the Pancho Villa character escaped. A boy or girl wearing a stovepipe hat typical of a revolutionary era politician would recite a speech that was once delivered by the martyred president Madero. The fiesta audience applauded the child's effort, even though he or she might have stumbled over the words. But the mere mention of one revolutionary figure—Emiliano Zapata—silenced even the wildest fiesta. Upon hearing Zapata's name, people young and old bowed their heads in deep respect.

Emiliano Zapata was the Revolution's shining star. Unselfish, completely devoted to his followers, and fearless in battle, he is regarded as the upheaval's greatest leader. So heroic is the spirit of the man that among the campesinos in the south he never really died. As the decades dimmed the memory of the Revolution, he was still seen, a dreamlike figure, galloping a white horse over country roads. His invincibility could be sensed in the twilight, around a fire where the old people gathered; it could be heard in their whispered words: "Yes, I saw him last night. I saw our 'Miliano. He was riding alone."

The Monument to the Revolution in Mexico City is the resting place of five leaders: Villa, Madero, Carranza, Calles, and Cárdenas.

CHRONOLOGY OF THE MEXICAN REVOLUTION

■ 1909 ■

Mexico is at peace. Porfirio Díaz has ruled as president for most of the previous 33 years. Díaz has brought factories and a modern railroad system to Mexico, but his policies allow land-rich haciendas to expand at the expense of village ejidos. Despite the country's industrial progress, most Mexicans remain impoverished and uneducated.

■ 1910 ■

April—Francisco Madero formally enters the presidential race. Madero is the first serious opposition candidate that Díaz has ever faced.

June—Díaz has Madero jailed on trumped-up charges.

June—Díaz wins the presidential election with a large majority of the vote.

September—A huge parade is staged in Mexico City to celebrate the 100th year of Mexico's independence from Spain. The crowd watching the parade greets President Díaz's car with icy silence.

October—Madero, recently released from jail, announces the Plan of San Luis Potosí. The plan declares the Díaz election to be illegal and calls for Mexicans to rebel on November 20.

November—The rebellion urged by Madero fails to take place. But two totally separate armed revolutions break out in the north and the south. In the north, Pancho Villa's army begins raiding rich cattle ranches. In the south the peasant leader Emiliano Zapata rallies landless farmers and takes over large haciendas.

■ 1911 ■

May—Pancho Villa, a Madero supporter, captures the border city of Ciudad Juárez. The taking of Ciudad Juárez is decisive because it allows Villa to supply his army with modern weapons purchased in the United States.

May—In Mexico City, President Díaz resigns from office and leaves Mexico for exile in France.

June—Madero enters Mexico City and is greeted by wildly cheering crowds.

October—In Mexico's first free election in decades, Madero is swept into office with a vast majority of the votes.

November—Emiliano Zapata issues the Plan of Ayala, which calls for the return of all village land taken illegally by the haciendas. Zapata denounces Madero as "an enemy of the Revolution" because he has moved too slowly on the issue of land reform.

■ 1912 ■

March—Pascual Orozco, a onetime ally of Pancho Villa, begins a rebellion against Madero. Madero elects General Victoriano Huerta to defeat Orozco.

June–July—Madero is accused of being antibusiness by the business community and of being turncoat by the revolutionaries. He is also attacked by the newspapers, which claim he is unfit to govern.

■ 1913 ■

February—The Ten Tragic Days begin in Mexico City. Artillery bombardments cause thousands of casualties as General Felix Díaz, a nephew of Porfirio Díaz, attempts to force Madero out of office.

February—As the fighting rages in Mexico City, Henry Lane Wilson, the American ambassador to Mexico, helps to arrange secret meetings between Felix Díaz and General Huerta. The object of the meetings is the overthrow of President Madero.

February—Madero is arrested by Huerta's officers, and he and Vice President Pino Suárez are murdered. Huerta assumes command of the nation.

October–November—In the north rebel armies gather under Pancho Villa, Carranza, and Alvaro Obregón. A war against Huerta begins.

■ 1914 ■

April—American marines occupy the port city of Veracruz. The marines remain in Veracruz for seven months.

July—Surrounded by revolutionary armies, Huerta resigns and slips out of Mexico.

August—Mexico City is occupied, first by the armies of Obregón and Carranza and later by troops loyal to Villa and Zapata. Villa's men begin a drunken rampage, raping women, looting stores, and killing indiscriminately.

■ 1915 ■

February—Obregón and Carranza reoccupy Mexico City. Carranza assumes political leadership over the nation. A war between rival generals begins.

April—The bloodiest battle of the Revolution takes place near the city of Celaya, where Obregón's army routs the forces of Pancho Villa.

October—American president Woodrow Wilson recognizes Carranza as the official president of Mexico. Wilson's move infuriates Pancho Villa.

■ 1916 ■

March—Pancho Villa and about 500 followers cross the American border and raid the city of Columbus, New Mexico, killing 16 Americans. President Wilson responds by sending an army under General John Pershing into Mexico with orders to capture Villa "alive or dead."

■ 1917 ■

January—General Pershing withdraws from Mexico after ten months, unable to capture the elusive Pancho Villa.

February—A convention meeting in the city of Querétaro approves a new constitution. The constitution calls for the separation of church and state, and it guarantees rights for workers.

March—Carranza is officially elected president of Mexico.

■ 1918 ■

While the generals of the north fight one another, Emiliano Zapata organizes a separate society in southern Mexico. The Zapatistas practice their own form of land redistribution by taking over large haciendas and dividing up the properties. Carranza sends army units to crush the Zapatista movement.

■ 1919 ■

April—Emiliano Zapata is tricked into attending a secret meeting with a Carranza general and is murdered.

■ 1920 ■

May—President Carranza is killed near the city of Veracruz while he is trying to gather an army.

September—Obregón is elected president of Mexico. Most historians consider that the ascension of Obregón to the presidency marks the end of the violent stage of the Mexican Revolution.

GRAL. FRANCISCO VILLA   GRAL. JOHN PERSHING

A rare photo of Pancho Villa and General John Pershing, taken before Villa became the object of a massive manhunt

Biographical Sketches of the Mexican Revolution

Carranza, Venustiano (1859–1920)—Carranza was born in the northern state of Coahuila to a wealthy landholding family. He served as a revolutionary general but was more a politician than a military leader. He assumed leadership of the government after Huerta fled the country in 1914 and was elected president in March 1917. Never a popular leader, Carranza was forced out of office and was murdered while trying to raise a personal army.

Díaz, Porfirio (1830–1915)—Díaz was born of mostly Indian parents in the city of Oaxaca. At an early age he joined the army, where he quickly rose to the rank of general. Through military manipulations he became president of Mexico in 1877. Except for one four-year period, Díaz held office for 34 years. During his time as president, Mexico made great progress in building railroads and factories. He also brought political peace to the nation. But Díaz allowed large landowners to usurp land owned by Indian villages. He did little to improve education. Díaz was forced to resign as president in May 1911 as revolutionary fervor swept the nation.

Huerta, Victoriano (1854–1916)—Huerta was born in the state of Jalisco to Huichol Indian parents. Though he was impoverished as a youth, Huerta managed to enter military college, where he was a brilliant student. As an army officer he ruthlessly suppressed several uprisings by Maya Indians in the state of Yucatán. In February 1913, President Francisco Madero asked Huerta to defeat a rebellion led by Felix Díaz, nephew of ex-president Porfirio Díaz. Huerta obeyed Madero's order but then cut a deal with Felix Díaz. The deal allowed Huerta to become president of Mexico. Huerta was an alcoholic and a drug user. Chaos reigned during his 16-month term in office. With revolutionary armies surrounding Mexico City, Huerta fled the country in July 1914.

Madero, Francisco (1873–1913)—Madero was born in the northern state of Coahuila to a wealthy and politically powerful family. He was a nondrinker, a nonsmoker, and a vegetarian. He believed in a spiritual form of religion and claimed he could speak to the souls of long-dead people. In November 1911 Madero became Mexico's first freely elected president in more than 40 years. But he inherited a land in the grip of revolution. Madero, a gentle, trusting man, was unable to govern the nation. He was arrested by army officers allied with General Huerta and was assassinated.

Obregón, Alvaro (1880–1928)—Obregón was born in the northern state of Sonora to a middle-class farm family. He became a revolutionary after Francisco Madero was murdered. Building his army around fearless Yaqui Indian troops, Obregón occupied Mexico City in August 1914. In the spring and summer of 1915, when the Revolution had deteriorated to its general versus general stage, Obregón defeated the forces of Pancho Villa in a series of decisive battles. Obregón became president in September of 1920, and he brought order to a land battered by ten years of revolutionary violence. He was assassinated on July 17, 1928, by a Catholic fanatic named José de León Toral.

Rivera, Diego (1886–1957)—Diego Rivera was born in the city of Guanajuato and as a boy displayed amazing artistic gifts. He spent most of the revolutionary years studying and painting in Europe. When he returned to Mexico in 1921, he became the most famous of the nation's "Big Three" muralists, the others being David Siqueiros and José Clemente Orozco. When painting historical murals, Rivera depicted pre–Columbian life as a lost Eden. The Mexican masses adored Rivera much the way Americans revere a movie star.

Vasconcelos, José (1882–1959)—Vasconcelos was born in the state of Oaxaca, where he studied law. Under President Alvaro Obregón, Vasconcelos became a cultural czar over Mexico. He sponsored the muralists who painted brilliant scenes on the walls of public buildings. As secretary of education he built thousands of public schools in rural areas and promoted teacher training. Later in life he established himself as Mexico's greatest intellectual by writing several books on Latin American culture.

Villa, Francisco (Pancho) (1877–1923)—Born Doroteo Arango in the northern state of Durango, Villa changed his name as a young man when he joined a bandit gang. Was Villa a genuine revolutionary hero, or was he a common thug? Mexican historians have wrestled with that question ever since the Revolution. He was known to kill men and rape women, seemingly without a second thought. Yet he often distributed food to the poor, and he set up schools in the territories he controlled. He remains Mexico's most controversial revolutionary leader.

Wilson, Henry Lane (1857–1932)—Henry Lane Wilson was born to a wealthy family in Indiana. He served as America's ambassador to Mexico from 1909 to 1913. A corporate lawyer, Wilson believed his primary goal was to protect American businesses operating in Mexico. Wilson's backstage maneuverings helped Huerta topple the government of President Madero. When Madero was arrested by Huerta, Wilson refused to use his influence to save the president's life.

Zapata, Emiliano (1879–1919)—Born in the southern state of Morelos, Zapata worked as a horse trainer and as a trick rider in rodeo shows. As a young man he watched with horror as the local hacienda owner took over land that had belonged to his village for centuries. In November 1911, he issued the Plan of Ayala, which called for land redistribution. Zapata recruited landless farmers and formed a powerful revolutionary army. Mexicans today revere Zapata as the greatest leader in the 1910–1920 Revolution.

For Further Information

Brandenberg, Frank. *The Making of Modern Mexico.* Englewood Cliffs, N.J.: Prentice Hall, 1964.

Brenner, Anita. *The Wind That Swept Mexico.* Austin, Tex.: University of Texas Press, 1943.

Cumberland, Charles. *Mexican Revolution (The Constitutionalist Years).* Austin, Tex.: University of Texas Press, 1974.

Fehrenbach, T. R. *Fire and Blood: A History of Mexico.* New York: Macmillan Publishing Co., 1973.

Kandell, Jonathan. *La Capital: The Biography of Mexico City.* New York: Random House, 1988.

Knight, Alan. *The Mexican Revolution.* Vols. 1 and 2. London: Cambridge University Press, 1986.

Parkes, Henry Bamford. *A History of Mexico*. Boston:
    Houghton Mifflin Co., 1938.

Reed, John. *Insurgent Mexico*. New York: International
    Publishers, 1984.

Ruiz, Ramon Edwardo. *The Great Rebellion, Mexico:
    1905–1924*. New York: W. W. Norton Co., 1980.

Turner, John Kenneth. *Barbarous Mexico*. Austin, Tex.:
    University of Texas Press, 1969.

Wilkie, James W., and Albert Michaels. *Revolution in
    Mexico: Years of Upheaval, 1910–1940*. Tucson, Ariz.:
    University of Arizona Press, 1984.

Womack, John, Jr. *Zapata and the Mexican Revolution*.
    New York: Alfred A. Knopf, 1969.

Index

A

Aguascalientes (city), 96, 113
Alameda Park, 26
American Civil War, 128, 137
American Revolution, 138
Arizona, 78, 109
Aztec Indians, 7, 9, 10, 32, 40, 58
Azuela, Mariano, 127-128

B

Barbarous Mexico, 128
Bierce, Ambrose, 128, 129
Bonillas, Ignacio, 117, 118

C

California, 78
Calles, Plutarco Elías, 139-142
Cárdenas, Cuauhtémoc, 142
Cárdenas, Lázaro, 142
Carranza, Venustiano, 71-73, 84, 85,
    89, 91, 92, 96, 99, 100, 102, 105,
    107, 112-115, 117-119, 122, 127
Catholic church, 17, 69-71, 97, 99,
    114, 126, 129, 134, 139-141
Celaya (town), 102, 103
Chapultepec Park, 57
Chihuahua (city), 36
Chihuahua (state), 17, 33, 52, 68
científicos, 22, 23, 26, 31, 38
Citadel, 58-60, 63
Ciudad Juárez (city), 36, 37, 38, 81, 82
class system:
    Indians, 9, 10, 16, 17, 23, 33, 40,
        52, 69, 129, 133, 138
    mestizos, 9, 13, 23, 33, 36, 73, 80,
        129, 133, 138
    whites of Spanish heritage, 9, 36,
        133, 138
Coahuila (state), 28, 71

Columbus

Columbus, New Mexico, 107
communism, 60, 125, 128, 130, 133,
    134, 138
Confederación Regional Obrera
    Mejicana (CROM), 124, 125
Constitutionalists, 73, 76, 78, 88,
    92, 113
Corral, Ramón, 19, 31, 38
Cortés, Hernán, 9
Creel family, 52
Creelman, James, 27, 28
Cristero Rebellion, 141

D

Decena Trágica (Ten Tragic Days), 58,
    61, 63
democracy, 13, 14, 42, 44-46, 68, 75
Díaz, Felix, 56-61, 63, 68, 124
Díaz, Porfirio, 13-17, 19, 22-24,
    26-29, 31, 32, 34, 37-39, 45,
    46, 48, 50, 52, 56, 68, 70, 72,
    106, 115, 137
Dolores (town), 31
Domínguez, Belisario, 69
Dorados, 82, 90, 92, 103, 105

E

ejidos, 16, 17, 22, 47, 50, 86
El Paso, Texas, 37

F

Fierro, Rodolfo, 90
French occupation of Mexico, 13
French Revolution, 138

G

González, Abraham, 68
González, Pablo, 105, 106, 115, 116

Grand Opera House, 26
Grito de Dolores, 31
Guajardo, Jesús, 116, 117

H

haciendas, 16, 17, 20-22, 27, 31,
    36, 44-48, 50, 51, 72, 84, 86,
    90, 105, 113, 116, 124, 142
Hearst, William Randolph, 17
Herrera, Rodolfo, 119
Hidalgo (state), 17
Hidalgo, Miguel, 31
Huerta, Victoriano, 52, 54, 58-61,
    63-65, 68-73, 75-78, 81, 84, 86,
    87, 89, 90, 92, 94, 96, 100, 106

J

Juárez, Benito, 13, 70

K

Kahlo, Frida, 133

L

Labyrinth of Solitude, The, 138, 139
Lascuráin, Pedro, 64
León (city), 105
León de la Barra, Francisco, 38, 43, 48
Limantour, José, 22, 31, 38
Lind, John, 76

M

Madero, Francisco, 28, 29, 31-33,
    36-40, 42-46, 50-52, 54, 56,
    58-61, 63-65, 68, 70-72, 75, 81,
    95, 100, 127, 143
Madero, Gustavo, 45, 57, 60, 61, 63
Madero, Sara, 64
Mexican artists and muralists, 129-134,
    141
Mexican literature, 127
Mexico:
  children in, 101, 103, 143
  Constitution of, 113-115

education in, 70, 114, 115, 125,
    126, 139
foreign businesses in, 23, 60
industrialization of, 13, 14, 15, 16,
    22, 24
women in, 87-89, 99, 101, 103, 133
Mexico City (capital of Mexico), 9, 14,
    24, 26, 28, 31, 34, 37-39, 45, 47,
    51, 52, 57, 59-61, 63, 65, 69, 72,
    73, 77, 86, 87, 90-92, 94-97, 99,
    103, 105, 107, 112, 118, 119,
    130, 132, 134, 141
Morelos (state), 33, 34, 36, 38, 46-48,
    50, 99, 105, 106, 116, 124
Morones, Luis, 124

N

National Palace, 27, 38, 57, 58, 61, 98
New Mexico, 109
Nuevo León (state), 16

O

Oaxaca (state), 13, 20
Obregón, Alvaro, 72, 73, 83, 84, 92,
    94-96, 99, 100, 102, 103, 105,
    112, 118-120, 122, 124-126, 127,
    136, 139, 141, 142
Orozco, José Clemente, 129-131, 133,
    134
Orozco, Pascual, 52, 54
O'Shaughnessy, Edith, 86-87

P

Pact of the Embassy, 61
Paseo de la Reforma, 26, 27, 37, 97,
    119
Paz, Octavio, 6, 89, 138, 139
Pershing, John, 107, 109, 143
Pino Suárez, José María, 44, 61, 63-65
Pistola, María (María Arias), 96
Plan of Ayala, 50, 96, 105
Plan of Guadalupe, 71
Plan of San Luis Potosí, 32

Puebla (city), 32, 118, 119

Q

Querétaro (city), 113

R

Reed, John, 91, 128
Rivera, Diego, 130-133
Robles, Juvencio, 48
Roosevelt, Theodore, 24
Russian Revolution, 128

S

San Luis Potosí (city), 32
Santa Anna, Antonio, 12
Siqueiros, Alfaro, 129, 130, 133
soldaderas, 89, 91, 97, 143
Sonora, Mexico, 18, 19, 72, 118, 119
Spaniards, 9, 23, 58, 69, 72, 133
Spanish Conquest, 9, 69, 97, 129
Spanish Inquisition, 70

T

Taft, William Howard, 51, 75
Tampico (city), 9, 76, 77
Terrazas family, 52
Texas, 54, 77, 78, 92, 109
Torreón (city), 90
Turner, John Kenneth, 20, 128

U

Underdogs, The (Los de Abajo), 100,
    127
United States, 13, 37, 38, 73, 75-78,
    91, 92, 106, 107, 109, 110, 118,
    133, 137
United States war with Mexico (1846-
    1848), 13, 77, 78

V

Valle Nacional, 20
Vasconcelos, José, 126, 127, 129, 133
Veracruz (city), 16, 39, 77, 78, 96, 118
Villa, Pancho, 33, 36, 37, 38, 43, 52,
    70-73, 75, 80-82, 84, 85, 89-92,
    96-99, 102, 103, 105, 107, 109,
    112, 113, 123, 124, 127, 128,
    143
Villistas, 33, 34, 36, 37, 89, 90, 96, 97,
    99, 103, 105
Virgin of Guadalupe, 64, 97

W

War of Independence (1810-1820), 9,
    31
Wilson, Henry Lane, 51, 59-61, 63-65,
    75
Wilson, Woodrow, 75, 76, 77, 106,
    107, 109

Y

Yaqui Indians, 18, 19, 31, 72, 73, 84,
    92, 94, 102, 103
Year of Hunger in Mexico City, 101
Yucatán (state), 44

Z

Zacatecas (town), 17, 90, 91
Zapata, Emiliano, 33, 46, 47, 48, 50,
    73, 78, 86, 96-98, 100-102, 105,
    106, 112, 113, 115-117, 124, 143
Zapatistas, 33, 34, 36, 38, 48, 50, 86,
    90, 96, 97, 99, 101, 105, 106,
    112, 115, 116
Zimmermann, Arthur, 109, 110
Zócalo, 26, 27, 38, 39, 57-59, 70